MORE THAN CONQUERORS

By
George Munson

TEACH Services, Inc.
Brushton, New York

2007 08 09 10 11 12 · 5 4 3 2 1

Copyright © 2007 TEACH Services, Inc.
ISBN-13: 978-1-57258-481-5
ISBN-10: 1-57258-481-5
Library of Congress Control Number: 2007929915

Published by

TEACH Services, Inc.
www.TEACHServices.com

DEDICATION

To the memory of Samuel Munson and Henry Lyman, who sacrificed their lives in an effort to tell the gospel story to the people of Indonesia. Their story inspired many young people to come to Indonesia to do gospel mission work. Ralph Munson was moved to follow his cousin's example. He and his wife Carrie came to Sumatra in 1900. With their five children, they were not afraid to face the heartaches, diseases, and difficulties of mission service.

Samuel Munson

Henry Lyman

"Who shall separate us from the love of Christ? Shall tribulation, or distress, or persecution, or famine, or nakedness, or peril, or sword...Nay, in all these things we are MORE THAN CONQUERORS through Him that loved us."—Romans 8:35, 37

CONTENTS

GRATITUDE

We are grateful for the help of many people who have made the publishing of this story possible. To Myron Munson for the story of Samuel Munson and Henry Lyman; to Harold Munson for illustrating the many events in pen and ink; to Jane Murdoch-Igler for reading the manuscript and making suggestions. To Naomi Bowers-Munson who spent hours correcting the manuscript and layout of the picture pages. Finally, for the encouragement of our children who urged us to print and for the effort of our son, Glenn Munson, in arranging for publication of this book.

INTRODUCTION

Samuel held his baby, Sammie Junior, in his arms, kissed him on the forehead, and said, "I must leave now. I don't know if I will ever see you again, little one. God bless you." The missionary Samuel Munson stepped aboard the sailing vessel. He and fellow companion, Henry Lyman, were beginning an expedition to search for a suitable mission location, whether on the Nyas islands or among the tribal Bataks in the Toba lake area of Sumatra.

Missionary Samuel Munson

Hungry jungle travelers!

Chapter 1

JUNGLE AMBUSH

The early monsoon rains left the weary travelers drenched to the skin. All day long the party of mission explorers struggled with cutting their way through thick undergrowth, and pushed through rain-swollen creeks, clogged with huge boulders and slippery logs.

The hired coolies groaned as they carried large boxes and heavy bundles, grabbing jungle vines as they swung across rushing torrents. They thought, "How hard will it get?"

Suddenly, in the distance they heard a welcome sound, a village rooster crowing. Sijan, the group's translator, happily announced, "We are nearing Goeting village." Following the trail through the village garden, they came to the thatch-roofed guest house and gladly set down their heavy burdens under the eaves.

The leader, Samuel Munson, turned to a villager standing nearby and asked, "May we speak to the village Rajah (chief)?" The man nodded and said, "*Ya, Tuan* (Yes, Sir). I will call him."

As usual, a crowd of curious villagers and laughing children gathered around the strangers. The Rajah came hurrying down the path holding a banana frond to keep the rain off.

The two missionaries, Munson and Lyman, greeted him by touching their hearts, following local custom, and then they gave him a hearty handshake. Samuel spoke in broken Malay as he told of the hard journey and requested shelter for the night. He handed the chief a note from the Rajah of the village they had visited the day before. The chief read the note and smiled as he said, "Welcome to Goeting village. You may stay here with us tonight. Make yourselves comfortable, and I will send you hot rice for your evening meal." He motioned for the villagers to follow him into the twilight.

With grateful sighs the men turned to moving their bundles into the shelter. Henry Lyman helped the Chinese cook search the bundles for canned corned beef, hardtack, and beans. Others in the group headed for the stream to clean up and put on dry clothes. In a few minutes a villager came running with a load of bamboo sections filled with hot rice.

Following local custom, the two missionaries invited the Rajah to join the group and eat with them. When he arrived they all sat down on the grass mats that someone had put down to cover the dirt floor. They all looked at the beans and steaming rice with eagerness. Samuel asked Henry to offer grace, thanking God for the safe journey and for the gracious supply of good food. As they devoured the food they talked excitedly about their hard trip. The chief asked about conditions on the trail.

Then his face turned serious. "Gentlemen, your objective for this trip is commendable. But, did they not warn you at Tappanuly that there was war at Lake Toba? Just the other day three heavily armed men came back from the Toba area and told of tribal war among the Batak. So why are you going there at this time?"

Samuel Munson, the expedition leader, shifted on his mat and motioned for Sijan to translate for him. "Rajah Amani Bassir, we appreciate your concern for our safety. Before we left the government office at Tappanuly, we talked to Mr. Bennett, the District officer. He had just completed a trip to Toba Lake. He was aware of the situation and expressed concern. We assured him that our objective was totally peaceful. We told him that the villagers would not resent our presence since we had come to help the people of Sumatra. Mr. Lyman and I are confident that God will protect us."

The two missionaries continued to question the Rajah about his people, their customs, religious beliefs and culture. They wanted to know more about the history and family life of the Batak people. After a lively discussion the chief noticed that the men were very tired, so he rose and dismissed himself by saying, "*Salamat Malem.*" (Good Night). The group prepared to retire and Samuel read a scripture and offered prayer. They realized that the next day would bring even greater challenges. The group was made up of two American missionaries of the Congregational church, a police runner supplied by Mr. Bennett, eight local baggage carriers, a Chinese cook and Sijan, the Mission translator. They had been asked by the Mission Board to search for a place to set up a mission station in Sumatra. They carried supplies for the trip and items for barter along the way. They were also armed with a musket and handgun to protect them from tiger attacks and encounters with the Sumatra rhino.

Early the next morning, Samuel was up writing a letter to his wife, Abigail, who was back in Batavia (now Jakarta), with Mrs. Lyman. They were anxiously waiting for their husbands to complete their expedition. In his letter he asked about the health of their baby boy who was born just six months before the men began their trip. He told her about the recent trek through the heavy jungle as they headed for Lake Toba. He mentioned the concern that the local chief had for their safety and that there was conflict in the Batak villages. Again he reminded her of their favorite Bible promise in Romans 8:35-37, "Who shall separate us from the love of Christ? Shall tribulation, or distress, persecution, or famine, or nakedness, peril, or sword? As it is written, for Thy sake we are killed all the day long, we are accounted as sheep for the slaughter. Nay, in all things we are more than conquerors through Him Who loved us." Signing his name with a flourish, he jumped up and called for the party to get ready for the trip to Sacca village.

As the hikers pushed through the jungle, they could not help but notice troops of macaque monkeys playing in the canopy of the trees. Large Sumatra hornbill birds danced among the branches. The sound of human voices and chopping of underbrush aroused the inhabitants of the forest. Orangutans, Sumatra's largest primates, sounded their deep-chested booming calls. Nearby, a Shama thrush, legendary king of the omen birds, warbled his beautiful song to his mate as she settled down on her nest. It was a glorious day in the Sumatra rain forest!

That morning, Samuel stepped over a fallen log and was surprised when a reticulated python slithered past his leg.

Someone had warned the group that there were cobras and other venomous reptiles in this forest, but they had seen no other snakes.

When the sun was overhead the group stopped for lunch, Sijan stepped over to a large jungle vine, pulled out his long knife and cut off several two-foot lengths for everyone. This vine stores drinkable water in its hollow core. Along with the usual fare of corned beef and hardtack, the cook had prepared rice balls. After he had finished his lunch, Samuel wandered over to the edge of the clearing nearby where he could see the tip of a volcano, he knew was on the Toba plateau. He asked the police runner if that was Mount Sibayak. These volcanoes are part of the "Great Ring of Fire" that surrounds the Pacific Ocean.

Samuel walked back to the group and said, "It would be nice to camp here, but we must move on to our destination." The men rose and eagerly pressed ahead, attacking with their knives the wall of thick vegetation.

About four o'clock that afternoon they came to a clearing in the jungle and stopped short. Before them was a formidable log barricade! Immediately, a warrior's head showed over the rampart. Everyone was startled and caught their breath as they looked at each other in dismay. The missionaries tried to explain their mission as Sijan offered a gift. Suddenly, a warrior shouted a command, and an ambush of two hundred men rushed up from behind the group, the baggage carriers dropped their bundles and fled into the jungle. In the confusion a warrior ran up to Samuel and sank a spear in his back. He fell mortally wounded, with a prayer on his lips. Lyman was shot with a musket and the Chinese cook was knifed to the ground. In the confusion, Sijan ran for cover in a bamboo clump. It was too late, three men lay dead in the jungle.

Chapter 2

THE DUNCAN SAILS

How did it happen that two young New England ministers from America find themselves trudging through the steaming jungles of Sumatra only to be cut down by native spear and musket? The story begins in nineteenth century New England.

Ten-year-old Samuel Munson was orphaned when the dreaded typhoid fever took the lives of his parents. A friend of his father opened his home to little Sam. He was a friendly boy and his playmates always welcomed him to their games. His teachers appreciated his sense of fairness and application to his work. He became a Christian at the age of nineteen and studied at the Academy in Farmington. Then in 1825 he began a course of study at Bowdoin College. He was known in school as being original and imaginative.

He was interested in preparing for the ministry, so he enrolled at Andover Seminary. It was at this school that he met a young man who later became his fellow worker.

Henry Lyman was attending the same seminary as Samuel, but he had a troubled spirit. He had enrolled there in September, 1825. He was easily influenced, loved to be popular, did not feel that he should be taking the ministerial course. Earlier, because of the death of a sibling, his father had dedicated Henry to the gospel ministry. Henry did not understand why he should be forced to take the course against his will.

One day as a result of a revival that had taken place in the college, a group of students were praying with their teacher. Just then the door opened and six young men walked in. They were bold, hardened, notorious enemies of religion. The leader was Henry Lyman. As these youth joined the group, on their knees, Henry was shocked to hear his name mentioned in prayer. His own sister had been working on him, but he still held out against this influence for good.

At that time typhus fever broke out among the students of Andover. One of Henry's classmates died suddenly. Then Henry got the fever and was sent home. His sister stayed by his bedside, treating him and praying for him. After his recovery, he returned to college to continue studies. One day his friend Samuel invited him for a walk in the woods. They sat on a log and had a long conversation. After a school-wide session of prayer and fasting, Henry was fully converted. With much prayer and counsel from his friend, Samuel, he was convinced to continue his ministerial studies.

Both young men had been meeting with dedicated Christian youth who seriously wanted to fulfill the words of Jesus recorded in Matthew 28:19, "Go ye therefore, and teach all nations, baptizing them in the name of the Father, and of the Son, and of the Holy Ghost. Teaching them to observe all things whatsoever I have commanded you: and, lo, I am with you always, even unto the end of the world." Early in 1832, the two young men were ordained to the gospel ministry. They both attended classes in Boston to learn about the detection and treatment of tropical diseases. Some time in February of that year they were accepted for mission service by the American Board of Commissioners of Foreign Missions. Since the Board had sent several missionary families to Hawaii, they wanted Samuel and Henry to get married, sail for the Malay archipelago, and settle their wives in Java. Then after one year of orientation and language study, they would organize an expedition to explore the large islands of Sumatra and Borneo. The young men were to study the culture, history and language of several groups of nationals to determine their readiness to accept the Christian faith. Since these islands were governed by the Dutch and British colonial governments, they would work with the authorities of each area.

This ambitious project was to be financed by eighteen local New England congregations. On June 10, 1833, Samuel Munson and Henry Lyman and their new brides gathered with many of the members of these churches at the Bowdoin Church in Boston for their last Holy Communion service and for prayers of dedication. There were four couples who were leaving for mission service. Besides the Munsons and the Lymans, two other couples were to go to Siam (now Thailand), to begin mission activities in this Buddhist stronghold. The pastor who preached that day reminded the brave young missionaries that they were going to a dangerous area, that they may never return to their homes in America.

A solemn group of friends and families gathered at the docks of Boston harbor to bid them farewell.

As the missionaries boarded the brigantine, Captain Randolph greeted them cordially and showed them to their quarters, which were below deck. No rooms, just open space between the decks. Bare beams, large bags filled with straw for beds, and a bucket with a long rope attached, for the "shower." The young men had gotten some muslin and tacked it up for "privacy" curtains. The baggage for the trip was brought into the space and friends helped to make things comfortable. Church members had gifts of surprise packages for snacks, and even farm tools were swung aboard by the ship's davit. The first mate balked when one congregation brought a bulky house frame. It was too big for the ship which had a length of ninety feet and a beam of thirty-six feet.

Finally the four families were settled. All freight and baggage were stowed away. The bosun blew his whistle and all visitors were ushered ashore. There were calls of "Farewell" from the church members standing on the pier. As the ship sailed out to sea, the missionaries could hear their friends singing, "God Be With You 'Till We Meet Again."

All lines were cast off as the gangplank was brought aboard the ship. Slowly the little chartered vessel began to move away from the dock. The harbor launch, manned by husky sailors, rowing rhythmically, pulled the vessel out into the wind. Sailors ran up the ratlines to man the sails. The big square sails billowed out as the wind began to fill them. The wind stiffened, now the brave little ship with its precious cargo was gaining headway. As the helmsman steered the ship out of the harbor, the young missionaries stood at the rail, waving a final farewell. As they strained to catch a last glimpse of home, Captain Randolph joined them on the aft deck. During the conversation someone asked, "Captain, how long do you think it will take to reach the Indies?" He said, "It might take three months." Already the ladies were feeling dizzy as the ship gently rolled in the swells.

As the little ship got out into the open sea they met waves from the Atlantic that caused the ninety-foot vessel to roll. The ladies were seasick for two weeks. Like many missionary families in later times, they took several days to get used to the motion of the ship. Then when the ship stopped at a port they staggered around like drunk sailors!

After sailing south for a few days, the ship's lookout reported a strange sail on the horizon. The first mate got out his glass and reported that it was a black sail identifying the approaching ship as a privateer. Pirates still roamed the Caribbean in those days. Captain Randolph gave orders for the ship's company to prepare weapons for an attack. He also asked the missionaries to go below deck to their quarters. Here is the story from Henry Lyman's letter to his sister.

"They appeared to be heading straight for us, thirty or forty monsters of all colors, and languages and nations. To flee was impossible! All hands were called, our carronades (smaller cannons with 16-lb shot), musket and pistols were charged. After half an hour of anxious suspense, we saw them cross our bow and head and bear away, as we supposed, to the West Indies I shall never forget the appearance of their vessel. Black hull, black spars and black masks, fitting emblems of their moral character." The four young missionary couples had spent time below on their knees, pleading with God for His protection.

Since they could average only forty miles a day, it took two or three weeks to reach the harbor of Rio de Janeiro, Brazil. There they took on water and food supplies. As the little bark sailed out of the Rio harbor, the passengers noticed that the captain and crew were busy tying down all the ships' gear and freight. They were told that they expected bad weather that usually came as they made the dangerous passage around the Horn. Sometimes the wind would gust to 100 miles per hour! The young Christian couples prayed again for the protection of God's angels. To the surprise of

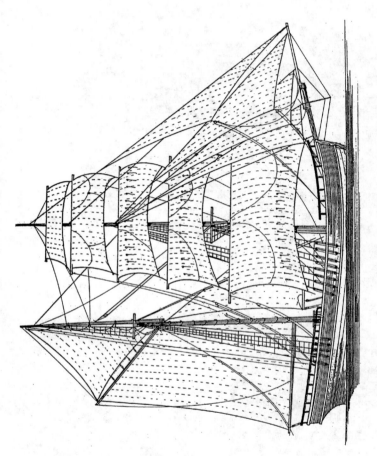

The brigantine "Duncan" was chartered to sail from Boston to Batavia, Java, with Captain Randolf and four young missionary couples aboard. The "Duncan" was 90 feet long with a beam of 36 feet.

The "Duncan" was approached by a pirate ship from the Caribbean. Its sails matched the black hull of the ship. They had heavy cannons and a desperate crew. They challenged Captain Randolph.

the captain and crew, the trip was calm and obeyed the Lord of the oceans.

Leaving the tip of the South American Continent, the voyagers headed across the vast expanse of the south Pacific ocean. As they headed west they passed many islands of the southern hemisphere and finally went between the tip of the Australian continent and the great island of New Guinea.

After one hundred days of sailing, the passengers and crew were glad to see the palm trees lining the shores of the islands of Timor, Flores, Sumbawa, Bali and Madura. At last the green island of Java appeared with its volcanoes rising in splendor behind the lush vegetation. After one hundred and five days, the little vessel cast its anchor in Batavia Bay.

The missionaries chattered excitedly as they saw the coconut palms waving in the gentle breeze and smelled the fragrance of exotic tropical flowers. This indeed was Indonesia!

The young couples went down to their "cabin" to finish packing and grab a bite to eat. Reverend Medhurst, of the London Mission Society, helped arrange for the hauling of baggage to customs at the government office. He called a becha (small horse-drawn cart). The group drove off wide-eyed, taking in the sights and smells of Batavia (now Jakarta).

When they arrived at the mission, the ladies especially took an interest in the houses that were to be their new homes. They were made of brick up to the windows, then woven bamboo to the thatched roof. Two mission families, the Munsons and the Lymans, were to stay in Indonesia. The Robinsons and the Johnsons were to continue in the chartered ship Duncan to Siam, where they would pioneer mission work.

They wrote to friends and family about geckos (lizards) walking on the ceiling. They noticed that these little lizards ate pesky mosquitoes and even the large, ugly cockroaches.

One delight of the new couples was to accompany their servants to the local market and learn the strange names of the exotic fruits and vegetables. "What is that large fruit with ugly thorns and strong smell, like rotten onions?" Durian! You break it open and eat the sweet custard-like cream on big seeds. The fruit they really liked was the mangosteen. It was as big as an orange but deep purple in color. A vendor cut one open and in the center was a snow-white fruit with sections like an orange that just melts in your mouth. What a fresh tart taste, like apple and rhubarb! They were surprised to see so many kinds of bananas and several different kinds of vegetables—bamboo shoots, mushrooms, watercress, coconut palm hearts, kangkong (like spinach that grows on water) and taro roots.

They were invited out to the homes of the Javanese, so curry and rice was familiar but what was that soy bean preparation they called "tempe"? During the many courses of these meals they asked questions about the new culture they were experiencing. Their new-found friends told them there were two hundred thousand Muslims, twenty thousand Chinese, mostly Buddhists, and about one thousand Dutch, mostly Catholic, with a small number of Americans.

They learned that around the seventh or eighth centuries Indian traders set up seven kingdoms in the islands fighting for supremacy.

Early in the sixteenth century Dutch explorers set up colonies and soon took over the whole archipelago.

The people were short in stature, with skin of a chestnut tone. In some islands, religions of Asia had deeply influenced their culture. The people of Bali, however, believed in a mixture of Hindu and Buddhist religions with a smattering of Animistic mores.

When the Munsons and the Lymans arrived they were advised to buy horses, the main means of travel in their day. They were encouraged to employ servants. Most expatriate homes had a cook, a house cleaner, a gardener, and a livestock keeper as well as a babysitter for any children.

The first year focused on language study (Malay and a dialect of Chinese) and orientation to the Asian life. Samuel and Henry received word from the Mission Board in Boston to organize an expedition to search for a suitable location to establish the first mission station. The Board encouraged an expedition to the Batoe and Nyas islands then on to the Batak tribe in Sumatra. Their quest would end on the big island of Borneo.

On February 27, 1834, Abigail Munson gave birth to their first child. They named him Samuel, after his father. This event brought great joy to the family and community.

The men were busy supervising the packing of food supplies, clothing, and other items for the expedition. They must not forget medical supplies, and always trinkets and knives to use in bartering for food and services along the way. They packed plenty of shotgun shells used in those days for currency. They carried one musket and a handgun for protection against wild animals like tigers and white rhinoceros.

On April 7, 1834, the mission group gathered for Holy Communion as they bid farewell to the two explorers. Samuel held his little boy in his arms: "Goodbye, little one. I don't know when I'll see you again." They boarded the vessel, Diedrick, leaving Batavia for the west coast of Sumatra. They noticed that their traveling companions were a colorful variety of ethnic backgrounds, speaking about a dozen languages. That evening the Chinese cook provided steamed rice with chicken stew, which would be the menu for several days, with occasional hardtack and corned beef.

Early on they sailed past the large volcanic island of Krakatoa. As they watched the smoke billow from its crater little did they realize that in just about fifty years that very mountain would erupt into an explosion that could be heard as far north as Shanghai, sending a tidal wave of more than eighty feet high to bury more than fifty villages on the nearby islands of Java and Sumatra, the third most devastating explosion in recorded history.

When their vessel stopped at Bencoolen to pick up cargo and offload goods, the men got off and visited the area. The British had built the city a century earlier but had turned it over to the Dutch in 1825.

The next coastal port was Padang, where they visited with two English missionary men, Mr. Ward and Mr. Benton. These men gave them expert advice about expeditionary travel.

At Padang the men transferred to a smaller eight-ton boat that touched at the small ports of the Batoe and Nyas islands, where the local chief wore just a loin cloth and the women of the village wore sarongs below the waist. In public they would throw a cloth over the shoulder. As they visited they found that a smallpox epidemic was decimating the coastal villages. These poor islanders needed a dedicated missionary doctor to provide medical care.

The Batoe islanders were very friendly but were caught in centuries of "indentured" slave trading. If a man owed a debt and could not pay the creditor, he was taken, tied up and sold to the Arab traders who in turn sold the poor fellow to the coal mines of Padang! Local feuds erupted as family members were lost to slavery. Though incensed over this situation, Samuel and Henry decided that this was no place to start a new Christian mission.

After finishing their investigation of the Batoe and Nyas islands, they sailed on the "Tajah" for Tappanuly. Henry was upset when he wrote to his sister, Hana, about the storm they encountered:

"We have slept aboard 40 nights. Everything is filthy, with roaches all over the boat. The men are bad navigators and very lazy."

They reached Tappanuly on June 17th. There, three people in the government office tried to dissuade them from making the trip to Lake Toba. The Baptist missionaries in Padang had told them that the Batak people were friendly to Christianity.

Samuel and Henry went to see Mr Bennett, the District Officer of Catholic persuasion. With kindness and courtesy, he did his best to persuade the two men to change their plans, sharing with them his experience on a recent trip to Toba where the people at Lobu Pining were at war. But the missionaries insisted: "Our mission is peaceful, and we are sure God will protect us from any danger." Mr. Bennett finally gave them permission to go and provided a police runner and eight baggage carriers.

The tragic end to the expedition is described in a letter sent by Mr. Bennett:

Tappanuly, July 2, 1834.

On the 17th of June there arrived here, on board the prau Tajah, Rev. Lyman and Munson, both American missionaries of reform persuasion....They requested my assistance in providing necessary guides, interpreters, coolies, and police runner who related the following tale:
'After their departure from Tappanuly they passed the first night in the village of Si-Boenga-boenga, at the house of Rajah Si Bloendae; the second night in the village of Rajah Swasa; the third in Pagerau Sambong, at the place of Rajah Goeroe Si Nonga; and from thence went to Goeting, to the house of Rajah Amani Bassir. All the chiefs received the men with hospitality and respect. These chieftains strongly advised them not to continue their journey any further towards Toba, saying that at Toba there existed disturbances...they remained firm till the 28th when again they prosecuted their journey from Goeting towards the village of Sacca, at Selingdong...proceeded on their march till 4:00 p.m. when suddenly they saw themselves surrounded by a band of about two hundred Bataks...and then inhumanely murdered Messrs. Lyman and Munson...the gentlemen themselves have been much to blame.'

Mr. Bennett could be expected to justify his actions since he had warned the men and the native chieftains had added their concern. Sijan, the mission translator, escaped from the attack and hid in the jungle and finally made his way back to report to the government and the Mission at Batavia. He told the grieving wives and mission director, Mr. Medhurst, that he was able to confirm that the bodies of the two American missionaries were dragged into the village and there was loud calling and rejoicing in the village throughout the night.

Later the Government found the mens' bones in a village garbage pit, and the Rhenish Mission buried them, placing a stone cross on the grave site, a memorial that remains there today.

Back in Batavia the local community and Mission collected funds and sent Mrs. Munson and baby Samuel with Mrs. Lyman to Singapore to await passage to Boston by the earliest ship.

Chapter 3

TOUGH DECISIONS

Ralph Waldo Munson was born in a very important period of American history. Both his father, Shubal Munson, and his grandfather, Eli Munson, were driven by an adventuresome spirit. Eli Munson had seen the first boat sail down the new Erie canal, headed for New York City. He marveled at the sight of the trial run of the first steam locomotive chugging along the banks of the Hudson river in 1829.

He loved to tell the story of his grandfather, who left the comforts of Seneca county, Ohio, in December of 1834. How the family, after many weary days of slow travel and a very dangerous crossing on ice of the Maumee river, arrived in Spencer county. He was surprised that his family were the only white settlers in the township. Grandfather Eli had moved into an area with eighty acres of virgin land. There was a huge forest of giant deciduous trees. Many oak trees measured five to ten feet in diameter.

He and his three older sons sharpened their tools and set out to build a log cabin before winter. It was only twelve by sixteen feet, with no windows, chimney or fireplace---too small for the whole family, but it was only a basic shelter.

The boys, Levi, Shubal, and Eli junior raised a good crop of wheat. While thrashing the grain they got an idea. Shubal suggested, "Let's build a haystack sleeping shelter!" They crafted a neat bedroom by arranging some rough oak boards in the middle of the straw stack, leaving a cozy cave to sleep in. They had a simple entrance covered with an old blanket. They slept warm that winter.

Ralph Waldo Munson, born on July 6, 1860 to Shubal and Electa Munson at Richfield Center, was raised in this little frontier town of Fulton County, Ohio.

While living with his family he developed a close relationship with his older brother Melvin, who was a cripple.

Many times he was seen in deep discussion with his sibling. Melvin was a devout Christian and at times appealed to Ralph to dedicate his life to God. The younger brother was reluctant to respond. One day Melvin got serious and reminded his brother of the tragedy that happened to cousin Samuel in Sumatra in 1834. He urged, "Ralph, you know that I cannot fulfill my desire to be a missionary to Batakland. Why don't you go there and teach those warriors about Jesus, the Prince of Peace?"

Ralph thought about his brother's words. One evening in March, 1876, he walked into a revival meeting at the local Methodist Episcopal Church. He was deeply impressed with the message and responded to the preacher's appeal and later was baptized. His friends urged him to enroll at Oberlin College in central Ohio, not far from his home in Toledo. He was told it was America's first co-educational school.

He attended the College and studied theology, majoring in journalism, which became an asset to him when he began mission service. He wrote for several mission journals and later learned to write in Malay.

While finishing his course at Oberlin, Ralph prayed that the Lord would help him find the right Christian young lady, willing to serve as a missionary in Asia. He longed to fulfill his brother Melvin's dream of preaching the gospel to the Batak people of Sumatra.

One evening he was leading a prayer meeting at the college for which Carrie Gassar, a student of the Conservatory of Music, was assigned to play the piano. She walked into the room and sat down at the back. Ralph was surprised when he saw her face, for this was the girl he had seen in a dream recently. After the service he introduced himself and later escorted her to the ladies' dorm.

They saw each other frequently. Carrie finished her music course, received her diploma and took an appointment to a school in Florida.

The couple continued to correspond and in 1886 they married. Ralph and Carrie were devout Christians and they really wanted to give their lives in mission service. Being Methodists, they were contacted by the Board of Missions of the Method-

Ralph asks Carrie to marry him.

Ralph and Carrie Munson

ist Episcopal Church and assigned to Rangoon, Burma (now Myanmar). They were inoculated for smallpox, cholera and diphtheria and given orientation to the tropical diseases such as amoebic dysentery, parasites and malaria. They got plenty of help in packing their personal effects so that they would not be broken. They needed to think about what they would need for the family for seven years or longer.

Ralph studied reports on missions and learned much about Burma. With passports in hand, steamer tickets purchased, and arrangements made for transportation to the port of departure, they were ready to go.

Family and friends gathered at dockside to bid farewell. With hugs and kisses, the couple said goodbye to the teary-eyed loved ones. The ship's steward ushered all visitors ashore. Sailors scurried around in preparing for departure. The couple stood at the rail waving goodbye to the crowd on the wharf as the steamer pulled away and the throb of the engines grew louder and faster and the city grew smaller in the distance.

As a scholar, Ralph was delighted to find a good library on board. He read to Carrie day in and day out the stories and history of Burma, her kings and ancient religious histo-

Ralph Munson and his wife Carrie joined the Methodist Mission and sailed
for Burma in 1886. He studied the language. Their first child, Miriam,
was born in Rangoon on October 7, 1887. A year later, while attending
a general meeting in Madras, India, they were assigned to the Nind
Orphanage in Singapore, Straits Settlement. He established a school for the
orphans.

ry. Every port of call was an opportunity to study geography firsthand. If the ship stayed long enough, they would take a bus or jinrikisha to see the exotic, teeming cities of Asia! Like all missionaries, their arrival was an exciting time, getting the baggage ready and going to the rail to see if anyone was there to meet the new couple from America.

It was such a thrill to meet their new mission friends as they were ushered through immigration and customs and finally to the Mission station. After all the excitement they settled into their humble quarters, attending orientation classes and the long-haul language study which, they found out, is a lifetime process!

Ralph learned that Burma has a long history and a high form of culture. Their architecture was amazingly complex and sophisticated. The language was written in Sanskrit. Learning to read the Bible was a real challenge.

On October 7, 1887, the Lord blessed Ralph and Carrie with a lovely baby girl they named Miriam. What a blessing to enjoy this little one!

During their first year of language study, they helped in the religious program and got acquainted with the national people. They attended a general mission meeting in Madras, India. At this meeting, they enjoyed the spiritual blessing. At this meeting the Mission leadership determined that Ralph's literary expertise was needed to start a school in Singapore-Straits Settlements. They were assigned to the Nind Orphanage in Singapore.

They returned to Rangoon and began to pack for the move to the new assignment. The trip by ship was short and in a few days they were settled in their new home on Sophia Hill, Singapore.

The little family settled into mission life. Ralph was given the task of establishing a school for the children of the orphanage. It was called the Nind Orphanage, after the Bishop who was in charge. Carrie taught music and Ralph taught other classes. He spent much time in language study.

It was here that three boys were born to the missionary family: Melvin, Albert and Paul. Later in life the children had fond memories of playing with the orphans during recess time.

One day trouble came to the orphanage. Young Melvin loved to run out to play ball with the school children during recess. It was his turn to bat the stick. He did so and ran out to the base. A mad dog from the village ran up to him and bit his leg severely. The animal was captured and was found to have rabies.

The family and Mission leaders were very perplexed. Doctors told them there was no vaccine in the area and that they had only 30 days to get Melvin to Paris. The Mission collected funds from the community and arranged for a nurse to take the boy to France. They boarded a ship and sailed for Europe. Bypassing India, they took the Suez Canal, through the Mediterranean and finally arrived in Paris.

Day by day young Melvin bravely endured the painful shots. He was the first American child to be treated by Louis Pasteur, and the French physician. The medical people were very interested in the case. Soon Melvin was released and declared cured! He could not wait to get back to Singapore. Upon his arrival, people marveled at this miracle of modern science that saved Melvin's life—half a world away!

The Munson family loved the people of Singapore and Malaysia. But ten years of exposure to malaria, tropical parasites and other tropical diseases took their toll on members of the family of four children. They needed medical care urgently. Carrie was suffering from a lung infection, the daughter showed symptoms of the same. The older boys had parasites and malaria, and young Paul was infected with amoebic dysentery. Finally, when Pappa was suffering from bleeding stomach ulcers, they were advised to go to the homeland for treatment. The family, with sad hearts, packed their goods and sailed for America.

Chapter 4

HEALING IN BATTLE CREEK

Ralph settled his family in Toledo, Ohio, where the Methodist Church had sent him to continue his ministry. Ralph went to Chicago, searching for doctors to find out what to do about his sick family. He walked into a health food store where he met a young man, George Stevens, who had been to Battle Creek, Michigan, and had been treated there. George urged him to go.

Returning to his family in Toledo, he wondered what to do. He walked into another health food store and again he met George who gave Ralph a ticket and urged him to take his family to Battle Creek. The family discussed the options and decided to send Pappa first.

When he arrived in Battle Creek, he walked directly to the Sanitarium. He puzzled over the word "Sanitarium." "Sanitorium" yes, but why that name? Later he learned that Dr Kellogg had coined the word. The place was huge and impressed Ralph. The doctors and nurses were kind and courteous Christians. The vegetarian food was delicious and the atmosphere gave him a feeling of security. He noticed that the workers were not shy in sharing their beliefs. In fact, the teaching of Christ's Second Coming was prominent on everyone's mind. One day he walked past the workers as they worshipped and was surprised to hear them sing a Methodist hymn.

His doctor advised him to spend a little time each day in the fresh air and sunshine. One day he was on the porch reading his Malay Bible. A nurse wheeled a patient out to the sundeck. He noticed that the lady looked like an influential individual. Soon they were sharing experiences. Ralph was surprised to learn that she had been a Methodist preacher and that she was the co-founder of the W.C.T.U. (Women's

Christian Temperance Union). She had worked with Francis Willard, the organization's founder.

The patient in the wheelchair introduced herself as Mrs. S.M.I. Henry, born in the Midwest and raised by a Methodist circuit riding preacher. As a child, she rode on the horse with him. Sometimes people invited them to stay or sometimes they found a clump of trees for shelter. She had memorized some of his sermons. This early training made her a strong worker for the Temperance movement.

One day Mrs. Henry noticed that Ralph was reading a foreign language Bible. He told her that it was a Malay scripture, called "Al Kitab." As they shared their experiences he told of serving as a missionary in Burma and Singapore.

He learned that she had just joined the Seventh-day Adventist church. They spent much time together, sharing doctrinal interests. She had studied with the hospital chaplain and was convinced that the Seventh-day Adventist church was following the Bible as the inspired Word of God. Ralph asked her many questions as they compared their belief of truths found in the Bible. Then she shared her story of healing that had taken place just recently.

Mrs. Henry was known at the hospital as a woman of prayer. Many times the hospital chaplain had called on her to join the staff in offering special prayer for seriously ill patients.

Mrs. Henry herself was suffering with a weakened heart. For more than two decades she had worked hard and was being treated for a heart problem. When a young lady requested special prayer and anointing, she joined the group to kneel in prayer. When it came time for her to pray, she pleaded with the Lord to spare this young lady's life, then she stopped, hesitated, then said, "Lord, please be merciful to both of us. Lay your hand of healing on us. Your will be done." Praise the Lord, He healed both ladies!

Mrs. Henry continued to study with Ralph Munson. One day she asked him, "Reverend Munson, what kind of a God do you worship? Is He an unmerciful tyrant who would give immortality to a sinner so that he could burn forever in hell?" Ralph thought that one over. When he realized that the Bible says, "All that do wickedly, shall be stubble, and the day that cometh shall burn them up, saith the Lord of Hosts, that is shall leave them neither root or branch, for they shall be ashes under your feet" (Malachi 4:1,4). That convinced him. As they studied the subject of "which is the true Bible Sabbath," he and Carrie were wanting to know what is Bible truth and not the traditions of the church. As Ralph talked with Mrs. Henry, he shared with her the feeling that he wanted to base his faith on Bible evidence. She showed him that nowhere in the Bible do Christians have a mandate to observe Sunday as God's holy day. He saw that Christ and His disciples observed the sacredness of the seventh day and that the apostles of the early church did the same. She showed him that back in the fourth century the Papal church made very fundamental changes during the Council of Nicaea. As a result they began to observe the first day of the week as well as refrain from work on Saturday. Eventually, the church emphasized the keeping of Sunday as a memorial of Jesus' resurrection.

Ralph returned to Toledo to share his studies with Carrie and his family. She and the older children agreed with him. They felt that for centuries, Christians had been following human tradition rather than the fourth commandment that God had given His church. They saw that God had solemnized the seventh day of the week when He declared in Genesis 2:2,3, "And on the seventh day God ended His work which He had made; and He rested on the seventh day from all His work which He had made, and God blessed the seventh day and sanctified it; because that in it He had rested from all His works He had made." The family studied many other related Bible passages and came to the conclusion that they had a serious decision to make. Mother Carrie turned to Pappa Ralph and she asked, "What are you going to do about it?" Resolutely, the whole family said, "We will obey the Word of God."

Before Ralph left the Battle Creek Sanitarium to get his family for treatments, Dr John Harvey Kellogg, leading physician at the center, had called Ralph and asked him to help with the work of the chaplain. He suggested that Ralph bring his whole family so that they might have medical treatment.

In those days the institution would treat missionaries without charge, no matter what denomination they were serving. The hospital would provide housing for them also. This was a real blessing for Ralph and Carrie.

The members of the family soon recovered and during the year Pappa worked in the chaplain's office, they became more acquainted with the leaders of the Adventist church. Ralph expressed his desire to be baptized by immersion and to join the Adventist ministry. He also had a keen desire to return to Asia as a missionary. He still wanted to go back to the Batak tribes and work for them.

Carrie was not so sure about taking the children back to Asia, exposing them again to tropical diseases. Lillian was born in 1898. She was a baby; how would this affect her health? Also, the older children would soon be needing an education. Together, they prayed earnestly about the problem, seeking the Lord's guidance. They decided to let the Lord guide the Mission Board and they would accept their decision.

With joyful hearts the family prepared to attend their first Adventist camp meeting. At that time the Grand Ledge Camp meeting was one of the largest groups to meet in the area. As they settled into their tent, they were impressed with the friendly campers and the spiritual atmosphere. They enjoyed the meetings, with lots of singing of familiar Christian hymns and powerful Biblical sermons delivered by inspired preachers. Many of them were pioneers of the Advent Movement, theologians in their own right.

The Michigan Conference had been supporting the establishment of a new mission effort in Ontario, Canada. That special project had gone so well that the church was ready to support another plan to open new work. Folks on the camp ground were talking about starting a new mission in Asia. They wanted to take up a special offering on Sabbath to sponsor overseas work. The church magazine, "The Review & Herald" gave this report on September 12, 1897.

"The Spirit of the Lord has been moving upon the hearts of the brethren in Michigan; and at this time they decided to select a missionary for a foreign field and sustain his work while there. Elder R. W. Munson, formerly a Methodist, who has lately come among us, spent several years as a missionary in Malaysia. He was on the camp ground, and cheerfully accepted the appointment to the Philippine Islands, and at the close of the meeting on Sunday, was ordained and set apart for that work. Earlier that week Ralph had been baptized by immersion along with a young German brother who also joined the church for service."

The Munson family went home to Sylvania, a suburb of Toledo, Ohio, singing the praises of their new faith and the prospect of mission service. Pappa organized the family in work teams as they prepared to pack for the journey and mission service.

Pastor Munson was willing to serve in the Philippines, but as he was praying about this new assignment he thought how much he would save the church if he could serve in a field where he already had a working knowledge of the Chinese and Malay languages. After some study, it was decided to send Ralph and Carrie to Indonesia where both languages were used, and he already understood the history and culture of the people. The Michigan Conference would help them get started and then he would become self-supporting.

Ralph was a careful packer. Every item was wrapped in paper and tucked in the best corner. Carrie supervised the packing of medical supplies for their proposed clinic. They knew that the people of Sumatra would need medical help. The children were excited about going back to meet new friends and the tropical fruits and foods they loved so much.

The packing was finally completed. Clothing and personal effects were in steamer trunks, medical supplies sealed in waterproof boxes; larger items were placed in crates. Pappa purchased tickets for the train trip to New York and passports and steamer tickets for the trip to Amsterdam, Holland. Since they were moving to a Dutch colony, they needed to get a knowledge of the Dutch language. Then they would take a ship and sail to Indonesia.

Chapter 5

PADANG ADVENTURES

The Munson family huddled under blankets on deck chairs as Pappa told them the exciting story of the two martyrs, Samuel Munson and fellow missionary, Henry Lyman. Then he read to them some of the stories he had written for mission magazines of the Methodist church. The family enjoyed watching the ships of many countries sailing by. They were headed down the English channel. The ship's captain pointed out the white cliffs of Dover and told them that the famous Bay of Biscay would be rough. They sailed past ships from France, England, Spain and Portugal. Once in a while a Dutch freighter or ships from Scandinavia would pass by. They were all plying the seven seas for world trade and maritime profit.

Soon they were passing the great rock of Gibraltar and entering the Mediterranean sea. Pappa was well versed in the history of countries that bordered this great sea. He reminded the children of the Bible account of the Tower of Babel and the scattering of the early civilization, breaking up into so many nations. How the Mesopotamian nations struggled for power. Assyria, Babylon, and Persia. The great Pharaohs of Egypt, and then Alexander the Great and his lightning strikes, bringing Greek culture to the world. The Roman politics, tough as steel. In the midst of this clash of power, the gentle ministry of Jesus Christ quietly slips into the scene, revealing the power of God in the streets and villages of Palestine. Of all the mighty conquerors who rose to power through the ages, Jesus' life and death and resurrection made the greatest impact on world history and culture! Soon He will come again in a blaze of glory to solve earth's serious problem of sin.

Ralph reminded the family that they were going to Padang to help Jesus finish His work in Indonesia.

As they entered the Suez Canal the sight of a caravan of camels trudging along the hot desert sand with the hazy

28

shadows of the great sand dunes of the desert lurking in the distance added to the excitement of the children.

They tried to imagine the huge congregation of Israelites being led by Moses through the Red Sea, across the burning sands into the desolate Sinai peninsula, and finally to worship God at the foot of Mount Horeb.

The azure blue waters of the Persian Gulf and the many small islands with a background of the vast Arabian desert called for exclamations of wonder.

Pappa took the children up to the captain's bridge as the ship corrected its course, to turn southeast and enter the royal blue waters of the great Indian ocean. The family knew that this was the last body of water to cross as they neared the great island of Sumatra.

It was a long trip from the skyscrapers of New York to the islands of the Dutch East Indies, and so the family speculated at lunch time. Would Sumatra be like Singapore?

Yes, maybe the streets would teem with men, women and children of many different races. What languages would they speak? Would they eat rice and curry or some other food from the jungle? As they were getting their dessert, they questioned the Indonesian waiter. What do the houses look like? What clothes do you wear in your home?

The captain came on deck and showed them the first sighting of the island of Sumatra, which was the headlands of Aceh. After many days of sailing from Europe to the islands, they were near the end of their trip. They went to bed that evening after watching the twinkling lights of the villages along the shores of Sumatra.

The children got up early and ran up the steps to the deck to watch the sailors dock their ship at little Emma Haven (today Telok Bayur) harbor. They tied up behind another ship taking on coal. They watched large metal containers filled with coal moving along overhead rails and dumping the fuel into the hold. Pappa called out, "Breakfast is ready, come and get it!"

After breakfast they all ran down to the cabin to pack their bags. The family of seven filed out to the deck, said good bye to the captain and carefully went down the gangway to the wharf. It was Sabbath and Ralph was wondering what he should do. A kind Dutch businessman stepped up and introduced himself. When he learned that Ralph and his family were American missionaries, he asked if he could help. He guided Ralph through customs and immigration. Then he offered to take them to a local hotel. However, the hotel cost too much for Ralph's budget so the Dutch friend gave him the name and address of a lady who would entertain the family. They called a couple of surreys and the family loaded up and started down the road to Padang. She invited them in and gave the family a warm welcome. She was a Christian, and they became close friends. They studied the Bible together, and later Anna was baptized as an Adventist Christian.

Anna was interested in the project that Ralph explained and suggested property that Ralph could buy for the mission school and housing for the family.

The family needed housing so they found a large thatched roof dwelling. This became their temporary home. Later, Ralph found a piece of property with two wooden frame buildings that were suitable for his family and mission work.

Ralph and Carrie took the children to visit the local market place. It was in a large brick building. There were so many vendors that the stalls of vegetables and tropical fruit spilled out onto the sidewalk. The children chatted about the fruit and begged Mamma to buy some. But Carrie was more interested in vegetables and grains for the table.

The vendors called out with sing-song notes advertising their wares. They talked to each other about the yellow hair, blue eyes and big noses of the foreign kids. Melvin called out to his mother, "Look at this pile of durian. I'm hungry for the fruit they have here. Let's get some for supper." The other children agreed and pointed to the large variety of bananas.

As the sunset began to glow in shimmering, golden rays across the Indian ocean, the family loved to walk barefoot on the beach looking for sea shells and pretty rocks. On Friday evenings they sang together vesper songs as they sat on the sand. Ralph and Carrie loved to plan interesting activities for the children. They would walk together along the Padang river and watch the fishermen bring in the catch. At other times

The Munson Family's First Home in Padang, Sumatra

The Family Loved the Fruits of Indonesia!
Pineapple, Mangosteen, Durian, Papaya, Rambutan, Banana, Pomello,
Langsat, Mango, Tarap, Breadfruit, Limes, Nagka, Laichee

Harold W. Munson '00

The largest fruit in the world, the Jack fruit or *Nagka*, weighs 50 lbs. After
taking off the outer membrane, the sweet, yellow pods with large seeds
inside are tasty, chewy morsels.

they packed a lunch and headed for Monkey Hill, which was across the river a few miles away.

One Sunday they planned a picnic. Miriam helped Mamma get a delicious lunch together. Young Albert grabbed a big hand of yellow bananas for dessert. When all was ready the whole family headed for their favourite picnic spot on Monkey Hill. At the crown of this hill was a rocky grotto. According to local tradition an old Muslim Hadji lived in that cave. The villagers brought food to him every day. He would share his food with a troop of monkeys that lived on the hill. The old man died, but the people of Padang still fed the monkeys.

On this outing, Albert was in such a hurry to beat everybody to the top he was huffing and puffing near the cave when suddenly the monkeys surrounded him. He raised the bananas over his head and shouted for help, as a big alpha male strode up to him, flashing his eyelid warning and baring his teeth. Albert shouted, "Pappa, help me!" The monkey grabbed the boy's pants in a threatening gesture. Father Ralph called back, "Throw the bananas into the bush!" With a burst of tears he heaved the beloved fruit to the monkeys and watched the feeding frenzy!

The Michigan Conference of Seventh-day Adventists contributed funds to pay for the Munson family to travel to Indonesia and purchase a home and property for a school and church. Since there was no budget for supporting a missionary family in Sumatra, Ralph and Carrie had agreed to serve as self-supporting missionaries. He learned in Singapore that English language schools and education were popular among the Chinese people. Also private English classes for business people were desirable, so this became their support base.

When the new school building was completed, the small company of believers used one classroom for worship and one for English language students. Soon fifty-three pupils were enrolled.

Not long after they arrived, Ralph and Carrie were shopping in town. A young Chinese man called to them, "Reverend Munson! Reverend Munson! Welcome to Padang." They turned to see who was calling. Lo and behold it was one of their orphan pupils from Singapore. They were happy to meet the youth. He told them that their former student in Singapore, Timothy Tay, was married and that he lived in Bukit Tingi a few miles to the north of Padang. Right away they wrote to him, asking him to come and help teach in the new school. They needed a teacher who had a working knowledge of English and understood Chinese culture.

Timothy Tay and his wife and child moved to Padang, found an apartment and soon were working with the Munson family in their mission projects.

As Timothy worked with the family he was eager to learn of their new understanding of the Bible. Ralph studied with him and soon Timothy wanted to be re-baptized, not by sprinkling but as Jesus was, by immersion. One Sabbath day they gathered on the beach near the Mission, and they sang together as Ralph baptized Timothy the second time, by the waters of the Indian ocean.

Ralph and Carrie were sensitive to the needs of the national population. They opened a little clinic to help the people with their medical needs. Soon, the whole team was busy helping in the clinic and keeping the school in order. Even teenage Miriam was helping her mother. Ralph could see that the Mission needed a nurse to help run the clinic, so he wrote urgent letters to Australia. Finally, a leader from the Australasian Union came to visit and determine the need for a nurse.

Here is the story in the *Review and Herald* of June 2, 1903. "Marcela Walker arrived from America. After her arrival, she was kept so busy attending to the sick that she hardly had time to study the language." The report goes on to relate that she and her helpers gave 307 treatments per month or an average of thirteen per day. Miss Walker had hardly enough time to eat her meals.

As Pastor Ralph Munson held evangelistic meetings, Miss Walker would present a health talk. This became an opening wedge for the Gospel. Even though the local doctors did not like the work of the Mission clinic, the results of prayer and the hydrotherapy treatments worked better than the drugs or the medicine man's charms. The patients realized the benefits. It also prepared the way for presenting Bible truth.

Since Timothy had been raised in the Nind Orphanage, he could speak English and Malay only. He knew very little of his native Haka dialect. He requested that he be sent to his native country, Amoy, China. Ralph agreed that he should do this, so he left for his ancestral home, Amoy. (His story appears in the *S.D.A. Encyclopedia*, page 268.)

In 1904 a young Chinese SDA, Timothy Tay, whom R. W. Munson had baptized in Singapore, went to Amoy (Xiamen), a seaport in South China, northeast of Canton, to perfect his knowledge of the local dialect so that he could work more effectively among the Amoyese immigrants in Singapore and in the Malay States. There he met a Chinese Protestant minister, Keh Ngo-pit (N. P. Keh), who in an attempt to prove to Tay from the Bible that the seventh day had been changed, himself became converted and joined the Seventh-day Adventist workers. Apparently Keh and Tay went to Swatow (Shant'ou), another seaport in South China where they preached to the Christians living there and where they made the acquaintance of a Chinese Christian leader, T. K. Ang, who also attempted to disprove the Seventh-day Adventist message only to accept it himself and enter the work.

When a large interest developed near the port city of Amoy in Fukien, to the north east of Canton, W. C. Hankins joined Keh and another national preacher there, settling near the city on the island of Kulang-hsu. The first inland station in the province of Fukien was established in the spring of 1905 at the village of Dongong (Dokong) some 30 miles from Amoy, where a national evangelist was put in charge of a meeting place. The brunt of the work was borne by nationals, some of whom went out preaching even before they were themselves baptized. For their benefit a training institute was held at Canton in December, 1905, the first of its kind.

Thus the work in Sumatra was helped as Timothy learned his mother tongue and the work in Southeast China was begun as well.

Chapter 6

CRISIS IN PADANG

Pastor Ralph Munson was concerned about the work of God in Sumatra. He wanted to expand his work and open a clinic in Medan, the capital city of Sumatra. He had traveled with the leaders of the Australian Union and they joined him in surveying the possibility of opening new work in other cities of Sumatra. But the Dutch government policies hindered this plan. Their request for permit to work in Medan was turned down.

During this time both Ralph and Carrie had suffered bouts of ill health. Carrie was sent to Bukit Tingi, where the temperature was cooler. Ralph had an attack of bleeding ulcers. At the same time he was concerned about his children who needed to be educated. Miriam was in her teens and Carrie was teaching her but she was so busy helping in translating at the clinic for Miss Walker, that Miriam's lessons were neglected. Yet the couple did not complain. They needed the help of more workers.

When Timothy Tay arrived back from Amoy, everyone was happy. Now he was able to speak the Hokien dialect of Chinese. One day he took the Munson children over to sing for his aging uncle. They brought a song book with them and the group sang for him. He was so delighted to hear the joyful voices of children that he wanted to learn more about the meaning of the words. So Timothy and Pastor Munson gave him Bible studies. Ralph was so happy to take this gentleman down to the sea and baptize him in the water as the first convert of the Church in Padang.

Another cause of rejoicing in Padang was the experience of a young Christian who visited the mission before the Munson family left Padang. He was Immanual Siregar, the son of a respected Batak minister. Let's read it in the Australasian *Record* of September 15, 1904, page 6.

"About a month before we left Padang, I was sitting one Sunday evening in my home, reading, when a Malay youth entered and introduced himself as a Christian Batak. I was very glad to see him and gave him a cordial welcome, for I had long been deeply interested in the work done by the Barmen (Rheinish Mission) in the uplands of north Sumatra, the land of the cannibal Bataks.

In the course of our conversation it soon became necessary for me to allude to the fact that we were Sabbath-keepers, and I went on very briefly to state the scripture of Genesis 2:1-3, that God had set aside the seventh day as a memorial of creation. He showed that when the Bible records the commandments it includes the phrase 'six days the Lord made heavens and the earth, and the sea and all that in them is, and rested the seventh day.' Nowhere in the Bible is there a record of any change to the first day of the week. Then in Matthew 5:17 Jesus said, 'Think not that I have come to destroy the law, or the prophets; but to fulfill. For verily I say unto you, Till heaven and earth pass away, one jot or one tittle shall in no wise pass from the law, till all be fulfilled.' Immanuel was convinced after reading several other verses (but he made up his mind to be very sure). So he went home to read his Batak Bible. He was in his early twenties. He had six Christian friends and brought them back to learn more about the Bible. When I gave him Bible studies on Daniel 2 and 7 he quickly comprehended all I said about the history of Babylon and the other kingdoms. He could read music, and used to sit for hours (at our Billhorn organ) and play sacred music. Just before we left he told me that when he first called, he came to convince me that Sunday was the Sabbath. It seems that the German missionary had told him, 'They keep Saturday like the Jews,' but when he heard the fourth commandment and studied the texts, his mouth was closed." Immanuel was Ralph Munson's first Batak convert.

Brother Immanuel Siregar became a strong worker and helped the members at Padang to trust in the Lord and let Him guide in their walk with God. He also helped to build up a congregation in his own home town of Tappanuly. The Providence that brought him to Padang against the advice of his father and the missionaries is remarkable.

Pastor Albert Munson, who followed in his father's footsteps as a missionary in Indonesia said, 'I remember how Immanuel Siregar met my father. It was 1904 when we lived in Kampong Debie. Immanuel was visiting with the Rheinish missionary when they told him about a Sabbath-keeping missionary, and so Immanuel came with a little lantern. (The police made all natives carry a lantern at night.) He came to show my father that Sunday was the true Sabbath, but after a few visits he became a Seventh-day Adventist and returned to Batakland to teach this message to his people." (From the Australasian Union *Record*, September 15, 1904.)

Immanuel was very sorry to learn that the Munson family was going to leave and go to Australia for medical treatment and education of the children. He spent much time with the family and used to sit down at Carrie's Billhorn organ and play hymns for hours. He did not want the family to leave, but in those days they couldn't get medical help near Padang, so they went to Australia. This left the little company of new believers without a shepherd. Pastor Munson said, "At our last service at the wharf there was weeping. They promised me that they would be meeting regularly at the home of Sister Anna every Sabbath day, and I in turn promised them that I would write to them and pray for them."

As Pastor Ralph left the shores of Sumatra, he had the satisfying feeling that he and his family had finally reached the Batak people. The future of the work in Indonesia would move ahead as God's people worked under the influence of the Holy Spirit. His desire to reach the people that his cousin Samuel tried so hard to contact was accomplished. The souls that God loved so much would find salvation in Jesus.

After the Munson family left in 1905, Immanuel returned to his home village and preached the truth as found in God's Word. He had already begun to keep the seventh-day Sabbath. He taught the people in his home village and had 21 people wanting to join the church. He brought his friends to visit the Mission and appealed to the leaders from Australia to send Batak youth to Singapore so that they could prepare to serve the church. Their names were: Immanuel, Gauis, Petrus, Hermanus, Simon and Hezekiel.

Elder Gates, administrator of the Union, was very pleased when he learned about these six young Bataks. This gave the workers an opening to reach the Batak people. Elder Gates decided to take three young men to Singapore. These men became good missionaries to their own people. This was Providential, for the Dutch government would not allow missionaries to work with the Batak population.

Not much was done in Padang after Ralph and Carrie left with their family until in 1907 when Brother and Sister G. A. Wanztlick of Queensland, Australia, came to Padang. They worked with the members who were not very motivated to witness and grow as a church. They had to search for former members. They were encouraged by the enthusiastic work of Immanuel Siregar, who worked in the Tappanuly area to present the gospel story to his family and friends back home.

Chapter 7

ADVENTURES DOWN UNDER

The Munson family arrived in Sydney after a very interesting trip by ship from Batavia, Java. They passed the island of Madura with its special culture of Sundanese. Then Bali with a very unique mixed culture of Buddhism and Hinduism. They found books in the ship's library telling about Komodo island, where huge dragons (lizards) measuring nine feet terrorized animals and people. Then they learned about the Lesser Sunday Island with very different cultures and terrain.

Soon the ship stopped at Port Darwin on the north west coast of Australia, where pearl divers have gathered the jewels for decades. They may have visited the old church where the names of pearl divers who had lost their lives were listed. The remains of an old and bulky diving suit that hung on the wall as well as a ship's bell commemorating victims of a historic cyclone were on exhibit.

They sailed through the narrow passage between the huge island of New Guinea and Australia's Cape York. Their ship headed south skirting the Great Barrier Reef. The children would have loved to go diving there, but instead the ship stopped at Brisbane, in Queensland, which was the famous center of the wool industry with thousands of sheep.

Arriving in Sydney harbour was exciting for the family. They saw the great harbour and largest city in the country. They found a very modern society, similar to home in Ohio.

After the usual immigration and customs details, they went by train to Cooranbong, where they were to make their home and attend school at Avondale.

At first Ralph settled his family in a little cottage near the school. They realized that they were in a different hemisphere, and the seasons were different from in the U.S. Also, the house was small, so Melvin and Albert slept out in a converted wood-

The Ralph Waldo Munson Family
Standing: Miriam, Albert, Melvin, Paul; Seated: Ralph, Lillian, Carrie

Catherine Innes and Miriam Munson

Woodsman Albert Munson with Axe

shed. It was winter time in new South Wales, so the family had to get warm clothing and bedding for everyone.

Albert was about fourteen or fifteen years old and to earn tuition and help the family with food money, he got a job working in the eucalyptus forest. He split railway ties and cut firewood. Melvin went out during vacation time and in the summer to sell books with the colporteurs. All the children helped in the home.

One day when Albert was working in the woods, he discovered a large Australian python that had retreated into a hollow log that he was cutting. As he looked over the situation, he noticed that there was a large sliver protruding out the end of the log. He went to the opposite end of the log and built a fire so that the smoke would drive the snake out on to the sliver. Sure enough, the snake slowly came out into the open. The teenager grabbed a limb and killed the serpent.

One hot summer day, Albert was working in the woods, cutting trees near Dora creek. He knew there was a deep pool not far away. Local boys liked to swim there. Suddenly, he heard a man calling for help so he ran to the pool and saw a man struggling in the water. Al pulled his shoes off and his outer clothes and dove in. The man had gone down for the last time. So the teenager had to make several dives, searching for the body. Finally, he came struggling to the surface with a limp body. Some people came to help pull the man out. They worked on him for an hour but he did not revive. The local doctor declared the man dead. Even though the man's life was not saved, it was determined that the man probably died of heart failure. Albert Munson was given a medal for doing everything right to save the man's life.

Both Miriam and Melvin, the two older children, had been sent to attend school in Australia in 1904. The next year the rest of the family left Padang. They were happy to be united again as a family in a little cottage near Dora creek.

Albert studied at Avondale thinking he would prepare to go back and continue his father's work in Indonesia. He had many friends at school. His sister was the friend of a young lady from Hornsby, named Catherine Innes, known as Katie, who visited Miriam in the home many times. Albert got acquainted with her as they attended school gatherings and picnics.

Father Ralph was busy at the publishing house in Wahroonga, working on translating books for the work in Malaysia and Indonesia. He also wrote articles for the Malay "Signs of The Times" magazine. Sometimes he held evangelistic meetings for the local conferences.

Mother Carrie was busy caring for the family needs, teaching piano and taking treatments for her lung problem.

One summer, Melvin took the train to Brisbane where he sold books to earn his tuition for college. He had purchased a bike and was riding on a gravel road down a long hill. Suddenly the fork on the front wheel broke and Melvin crashed headlong to the ground, lacerating his face. His face healed up, but the accident affected his health later on in life.

Melvin helped with evangelistic meetings held at Christ Church, New Zealand. He later studied journalism and his father encouraged him to write in Malay.

Miriam was a beautiful young lady in her late teens and had a very mellow contralto voice She was popular at the school and sang with musical groups. She also learned to play the piano from her talented mother, Carrie.

The Australasian Union Conference committee was interested in setting up a publishing house somewhere in Indonesia or Singapore. Ralph and Carrie Munson were asked to carry out this program. The place was Sukabumi—meaning "delightful hill." Pastor Ralph was praying that the government would give him permission to print religious literature. It was February, 1910. Arrangements had been made to purchase small equipment to start the project, but a permit from the governor was needed in order to print religious literature in Java. So Ralph made an appointment to visit him. He was greeted with extra kindness. Ralph presented their plan to publish Christian literature in the major languages of the Indonesian people. The governor told Ralph that he was a Christian and that he welcomed their project. He said he would try to expedite the granting of a permit and was happy to pray with Ralph.

Pastor Ralph was assisted by Brother Hungerford and several national brethren. A Mr. Lee came from Singapore to be the pressman; Immanuel Siregar, who was Pastor Ralph Munson's first convert from Batakland; and Samuel Rantung, from Minehasa, Celebes.

All worked together to provide literature for a growing force of colporteurs. They printed a quarterly, "Utusan Kebanaran Malayu." ("Messenger of Truth.") Several Malay tracts were printed as well as Ralph's translation of Elder G. B. Star's book entitled "Saksi Kebanarian," a series of Bible studies.

This printing plant continued to publish for a few years. Then the Mission decided to move the plant to Batavia (Jakarta) because the people of Sukabumi opposed their work.

In April, 1911, the Press was moved to Batavia. Ralph and Carrie were kept busy with the publishing work. Miriam was giving Bible studies to her Chinese friends and Melvin joined his parents to help with the editorial work in the new printing plant. They praised God for the progress in the printing work.

All was not well with the Munson family's health, so finally they decided to return to their home in Australia, where Albert was attending school. From there they packed up their belongings and returned to their homeland, America.

The beginning of the publishing work in Java strengthened the whole church in Indonesia and Malaysia. As a result of the economic growth in Singapore, this city became the headquarters of our mission work in Southeast Asia. After 1915, the headquarters of the Far Eastern Division were established there.

While finishing his education in America, Melvin got acquainted with a young lady named Irene Frisby. In 1917 they married and were called to be missionaries in Batavia. Melvin was to be editor of the Signs of The Times Publishing House, which was later moved to Singapore.

On January 4, 1918, a baby boy was born to them and they named him Eugene. Melvin's duties included working in several languages. He had a good staff of workers.

Tragedy struck Melvin's family when Irene gave birth to their second son, Ralph. She died after childbirth, but the baby lived. So, with two small boys, Melvin was forced to return to America. There he met Harriet Sherrill, whom he later married. Melvin's thoughts were always with the mission work that he had been connected with most of his life.

In 1923, Melvin received a call from Singapore to be editor of the Signs of the Times Publishing House of Malaysia. He wasted no time in going back to the work closest to his heart. A baby girl, Melva, was born to them, May 14, 1925, in Singapore. Again in 1927, Melvin had to leave his mission work for medical reasons. So they returned to America and settled in La Sierra, California.

In the early forties he was called by the U.S. government to join a group of people who knew the Indonesian language to write script to broadcast the "Voice of America" which was beamed by radio to the people of Indonesia. This gave the people hope during World War II.

Irene and Melvin Munson

Melvin with his two boys,
Ralph and Eugene

Melvin Munson Family
Back row, left to right: Eugene & Maxine; Melva, Lois & Ralph;
front: Harriet & Melvin

Chapter 8

ANGRY LEOPARD!

Catherine Innes had completed her nurse's course and set up a clinic for Midwifery. In fact, she had gotten a loan from her father to establish her own business. When she received Albert Munson's letter proposing marriage, she kept him waiting until she could settle her finances.

December 1, 1917, was a very happy day for Albert. Now he could take his Australian bride on their honeymoon to Java, the land of his dreams. When they arrived, Albert was dancing with delight to meet the Indonesian people. He could speak their language, revel in the taste of curry and rice, the taste of tropical fruits like durian, mangoes, sixteen varieties of bananas and the delicious mangosteen. Catherine was surprised by the strange sounds and smells and by people washing in filthy canals, or squatting down beside a roadside vendor eating their meals. She missed talking English. She used to say, "I cried the first year I was in Java." However, she later learned to love the people and culture of Indonesia.

George, their first son, was born in Soerabaya, Java, on October 22, 1918. The second son Harold was born November 8, 1920. Albert's mission duties kept him busy. Someone had to baby sit the little two-year-old, so he decided to take a short vacation at the mission cabin in Sumerwekas. The Mission kept a cabin for workers to rest from the malaria-ridden lowlands of East Java.

He packed a little suitcase and picking up the toddler went out to catch the bus for Pregen. Little Georgie was asking a string of questions. Native food vendors were trotting along the crowded streets calling out. "Ae-ro-tee, Ae-ro-tee!" cried out the bread vendor. Across the road a man shouted, "Pisang Goreng, Pisang Manis" (fried bananas, sweet bananas).

Ninety minutes later the bus rattled to a stop at the Pregen station. With George in his arms, Albert trudged down the path through the banana orchard to the cabin. As they turned the corner of the building a surprise met their eyes. A LEOPARD PELT!

Amin, the native caretaker came joyfully bounding out of the building. He said, "Slamat dating, Tuan!" ("Mister, you have come in peace.") He noticed Albert curiously eyeing the spotted skin. He turned and explained, "A couple of days ago this female leopard was visiting the forest behind the cabin and attacking the troop of monkeys living there. I decided to scare her off with the mission gun. One evening she was making a disturbance, so I grabbed the gun and went to see what was going on. I squatted beside a bush and looked around. I heard a crunching sound in the bush next to me and spotted this leopard chewing on a monkey. I raised the gun and fired. (I was so close I almost blew her head off.) The next day I skinned her, treated the pelt with salt and nailed it on that wall."

The leopard roared angrily! Each night he came out to the mission cabin which was built above the ground. Someone had killed his mate, skinned her, and nailed her pelt to the cabin wall! Daily he visited the site, reaching up to scratch the skin and growl his discontent. Then he would crawl under the house to continue his grumbling.

Albert was unhappy because his sleep was being disturbed by these nightly visits. That evening the animal returned to grumble and growl under the cabin, just below the bedroom. About five in the morning the leopard gave a loud roar that brought the missionary out of his bed with a bound. He staggered into the bathroom, mumbling threats to the beast under the house. On his way to the kitchen he checked on Georgie who was still asleep. He fried eggs and rice, finished his breakfast, went to the gun rack and loaded the weapon. All that was available was bird shot! He thought it would be foolish to try using such light shot but the blast would scare the animal away.

Stepping outside, he walked to the edge of the ravine to see where the creature had gone. As he looked across the canopy of the forest he spied a beautiful sight. There sitting on a limb was a male leopard with a gorgeous orange-yellow coat

Albert, Catherine, and little George

Surabaya Church

with black spots shining in the sun! How could he kill such a lovely creature? As he hesitated, he remembered the experience of the night before. He was sitting in front of the dormer window of the little round gazebo, waiting for the animal to visit the area. There he saw him, sneaking up the hill towards the house. Albert could hear the animal's breath whistle into his nostrils after one of those growls. Suddenly, a dead limb broke off the big durian tree growing beside the building and hit the tin roof with a loud crash. The missionary almost hit the ceiling, and the animal scrambled for cover.

Albert decided to give the leopard both barrels to give him a good scare. BANG! BANG! The sound echoed through the forest. When the smoke cleared, he noticed that the leopard turned and gave him a dirty look and started to come down the tree by jumping from limb to limb. Albert remembered reading about hunters in Africa being mauled after wounding a leopard. He headed for the cabin in great haste. He called for Amin and asked him to run down to the village and assemble some spearmen to capture the leopard. When the group finally assembled at the foot of the tree, they found that the animal had leaped twenty feet to the bank and headed in the opposite direction. They never found him! The missionary vowed he would never hurt a wild creature again.

Albert Munson learned the Malay language well and was able to work with the national workers to raise up new churches and care for the spiritual needs of the members. Wherever he traveled he held Bible studies, gathering the people in private homes. He set up his hand-drawn charts and taught the people the gospel truth.

Early in Albert's experience in Indonesia he learned about human relations. He had been given the responsibility of president of the East Java Mission, with headquarters in Soerabaya. He was much younger than the former leader who had other responsibilities. Because of differences of opinion about certain problems and procedures, unhappiness was generated between them.

One day Albert was walking home from a long trip by foot. The sun was very hot. He came to a roadside vendor of cool drinks. He could not resist. He paid a coin and drank the cool glass of water. It slaked his thirst, but several days later he came down with a high fever. The doctor said it was typhoid fever! Being a trained nurse, Catherine did her best to get his fever down, but to no avail. Both the high fever and administrative troubles worsened his condition.

Mumbling incoherently in his delirium, he begged his wife to throw cold water on him. Of course she refused and continued to sponge him to cool the burning fever. Finally he pleaded, "Call our missionary brother, I must make things right lest I die!" The missionary came, and they settled their misunderstanding. From that time on he improved. That evening he asked Katie to sing his favorite hymn, "Jesus is All the World to Me." She sat up to the little folding Billhorn organ and sang, "Jesus is all the world to me, my life, my joy, my all..." He was taken to the hospital and soon recovered to his full strength. The doctor told him he was a lucky man. He said that if he had been a drinker or smoker he would not have survived.

One of the Mission projects then was to build a decent church for the city of Soerabaya. In 1921 the Mission was assigned a goal for Ingathering. Albert requested that the overflow be assigned to the new headquarters church building fund. Albert diligently solicited funds among the rich Chinese people. Prior to this a Chinese layman had given Bible studies to a leading Chinese gentleman. He had three sons who were leading contractors in the city. The father was ill but had accepted the Christian faith. Before he died he advised his three sons to become Christians. Like good sons they studied the Christian faith and joined the church. Tan Sim Lok, Tan Sim Ho, and Tan Sim Look were involved in the planning for the Soerabaya church building project. They worked with Missionary Albert in the architectural plans and were involved in drawing up special specifications. They wanted to do the best job in providing a house of worship for God's people. Albert had visited the local businessmen and gotten good donations for the new church. The Tan brothers had agreed to be the main donors to this plan. They insisted that teak, the best wood, be used for doors, windows and pews. They themselves had donated marble for the platform and floor. They drew up plans for the baptistry. It was going to be a very special sanctuary. When dedicated, this church was the pride of the whole Mission. Little did they know that eighteen years later, when the Japanese Air Force bombed Soerabaya, this very church would be the scene of a miracle of God in World War II.

The ominous roar of flights of Japanese bombers terrified the city as sirens howled and bombs thundered. Blocks and blocks of buildings were razed. Houses were burning all around them as the pastor and his little family slipped into the church. They decided that the baptistry was the safest place to be. They huddled in the tiny space, listening to the conflagration outside. Much of the city had been destroyed and hundreds of people killed. The pastor's family began praying earnestly that God would send His angels to protect them. First the father, then the mother prayed. What a prayer meeting, in the baptistry! Young Christian, just twelve years old, remembered Psalms 34:7. Over and over he pleaded, "The angel of the Lord encampeth round about them that fear Him, and delivered them." Then his sister Ketty, who was four, prayed, "Dear Jesus, Thou hast promised to send Thine angels. Keep Thy promise. Oh, Jesus, send the angels!" So they prayed and the God of heaven heard. When all was quiet, the pastor went out to see if any fire had caught on the building. Two policemen met him with an angry group of people. They demanded to know, "Who was singing in your church just now?"

"Singing?" he said. "Singing? Nobody. The church has been empty." The police and the people did not believe him, so they went inside and found the place empty. They went away wondering.

Then the bombers returned. The engines roared louder and louder and then came the roar of the bombs. The city was being devastated. The pastor had been reminded that curfew laws were being enforced; there were to be no assemblies.

The little family hid in the baptistry again. While the bombers roared overhead, the people in the community could hear choir music coming from the church. This time the pastor and his family heard the beautiful music in the church. The all-clear sounded and then loud knocking on the church door. The pastor this time explained that he had heard the music He showed officials that only his family was huddled in the small space of the baptistry. He told police that he was sure it was a choir of angels, for he and his little family heard the angels singing the song, "All the way my Saviour leads me." They knew that God had sent His angels to protect them.

One year after the completion of the new church, a baby girl was born to the Munson home. Iva Nellie arrived on March 22, 1922. Albert and Catherine were overjoyed that the Lord had given them a daughter. The two brothers loved to hold their little sister. Later, they took too much delight in teasing her.

In 1923, Albert received word from the Malaysian Union that the leaders wanted him to pioneer a new mission project. An Adventist colporteur, Daniel Lim, had been giving Bible studies to a group of devoted Chinese people living on the island of Celebes (Sulawesi). This work needed to be followed up.

Since it was time for the family to go on furlough, Albert and Catherine planned to visit her family in Australia and then six months later visit his relatives in California. The children were excited that they would get to see Grandpa Innes' farm in Hornsby. Their mother had told them about her family in Australia. And after that, the United States was waiting to be explored.

The Albert Munson Family on Furlough

Harold, George and Iva were all born in Seorabaya, Java.

Visiting Grandpa and Grandma Innes in Australia

George and Sarah Innes
(Grandpa and Grandma Innes)

Chapter 9

FANTASTIC FURLOUGH

In the previous pages we learned about the family of Ralph Munson, Albert's father. So far we have relied on the memories of other people. Now we will tell the story of Albert's oldest son, George. He was born on October 22, 1918, in the city of Soerabaya, Java,

Visiting the maternal parents of his mother, Catherine Innes, was a unique experience, for the culture in Australia was different from Indonesia. It was new to the missionary family. Daily, for dinner, Grandma Sarah Innes served mashed potatoes and brown gravy, green peas, and beef sausages. For Christmas, there was a traditional English boiled pudding in which Grandma hid money. The children ate pudding until they found the prize!

When George was seven years old, and living with the family in the town of Hornsby, it was time for him to go to school. His mother bought for him a little leather backpack to carry his school books. Mother strapped the bag on his back and walked with him down the road to the pre-school, named Camelot College. He was scared to see so many white boys and girls. When he needed to go to the restroom he was too shy to ask the teacher so he wet his pants. What an awful embarrassment! He cried all the way home.

While going to this school he learned a lesson in math. He was working quietly on an addition problem and using his fingers to add a sum. The teacher caught him and with a whack on the hand with a ruler reminded him not to use his fingers. He quickly learned that fingers may be "digits" but not for math.

Good times came when George's siblings joined him in playing outside in Grandpa's milking stanchion. They imagined it was a ship. When the sun was hot Grandma brought three tall glasses of ice-cold lemonade, decorated and flavored with a mint leaf. That was so–o–o refreshing.

Uncle George, their mother's teen-aged younger brother, thought that missionary kids were pretty funny. One day he persuaded young George to borrow an old umbrella, climb onto Grandpa's barn roof and jump off for an exciting parachute ride! Foolishly he did it and landed in a heap on the hard ground! Uncle George got his punishment and his nephew lay in bed for a few days. Today, George's lower spine is crooked.

Grandma Sarah was a good teacher. She was a tiny Scottish lady with a big heart. She called George one day and asked him to help carry groceries from the Hornsby market. He trudged along beside her asking all kinds of questions. Where did Grandpa work? What was he doing in the city of Sydney? How did he get to work? She told him that Grandpa had been a "steeplejack." He did carpenter work and built houses. He could pound nails with either hand. When he worked high on a church steeple, he could use both hands to do his job. However, one day when he was working on a multistoried building, he slipped and fell down two stories landing on his side on a floor joist! When he recovered, he worked on lower buildings. He taught his two sons, Bill and George, how to build. His oldest son, Bill, could work on masonry and George did carpentry. The boys helped their father build six brick homes on their property at Hornsby. They dedicated one home to be used in helping people. Grandma told George that after lunch she would show him how she helped needy people.

After they had washed the lunch dishes Grandma took George to the special locker. They opened the lid of the box and on the right was a pile of carefully ironed clothes, and on the left were groceries. "George," she said, "Jesus wants us to share our goods with needy people." She put some clothes in one bag and groceries into another bag. Then they walked down Hall Road to the home of a needy family. Grandma introduced her grandson to the lady of the house and then gave them the food and clothing. They were very thankful for the help and George felt proud of his Grandma.

Father Albert loved to work in Grandpa's vegetable garden. He planted a large bed of radishes. They grew well and Albert ate so many it burned his tongue and it got red and hurt.

The three children loved to play in Grandpa's orchard. They collected windfall apples and stored them in little storage shelters they made with bricks lined with straw.

One day George had a very sore throat. His parents took him to the Sydney Sanitarium and had his throat examined. He needed to have his tonsils taken out. Going to the hospital for surgery was scary, but Doctor Harrison, an American physician, was very kind. He told George he was going to put a mask on him and asked him to count to twenty. He started to count but did not reach twenty. When he woke up his throat was very sore, but the kind nurse gave him some ice cream. That really helped.

The time came for the family to sail to California and spend the second half of their furlough with Grandpa and Grandma Munson. They packed their bags and took the train to Sydney. Arriving there, they went to the dock where the big ocean liner, "Aurangi," was berthed. The whole Innes family came to say goodbye. Grandma, bless her heart, had secretly packed a special surprise box for the grandchildren. They were instructed to open a section of this box every day of the journey! Grandpa had packed a lug box of Bartlett pears from his orchard. When they got yellow they were delicious!

Besides their usual baggage, this family had strange cargo aboard. Away up on the boat deck was a crate of large red chickens, called Australorp hens, and a big red rooster, called Big Ben. They were being fed by the family. Melvin's wife Harriet loved to work with chickens. When she learned Albert was going to visit the "fuzzy-wuzzy" natives of New Guinea, she requested that he bring her the skins of four exotic birds—two golden birds of Paradise and two rare passenger pigeons (and the Australorp) chickens. In those days, ladies wore exotic bird feathers on their hats!

The trip up the eastern part of the Pacific was not very interesting because the ship did not stop at Chilean or Peruvian ports. A stop at Mexico and other countries would have been interesting.

The journey came to an end. Upon awakening the next morning, they saw that their ship had arrived in San Pedro,

Los Angeles. The kids ran up on deck to watch them weigh anchor and dock the ship.

Their Munson grandparents lived in Pomona where Grandpa was pastor of the old Victorian church. Their furlough was for only six months. Those were memorable days as they played with their cousins who came to visit with the family. Uncle Clarence and Aunt Lillian Spaulding came from Colorado. Their children were Elwyn, Ruth, Rose and Jean. Aunt Miriam and Uncle Ernest Brown lived nearby. Eugene and Ralph and Melva visited from their home in La Sierra. Cousin Margaret entertained them with her skill on new roller skates.

Grandma Carrie Munson was an accomplished pianist, having finished the conservatory of music at Oberlin College, Ohio. She gave them piano lessons and Margaret gained the biggest blessing from that summer. George never succeeded beyond playing "Chopsticks" with one finger.

When the cousins get together now they joke about Grandpa Ralph's funny habits. He came home late in the evening, cut up some cold baked potatoes in a dish, poured honey on it and enjoyed the stuff. Then we could hear him mix a cup of cocoa, rattling the spoon in his tin cup!

On Sabbath morning when Grandpa Ralph was ready for church, he went to the old barn of a garage, cranked up the Model T Ford, drove it out to the curb in front of the house and started honking. "Auugah, AUUGAH!"

Carrie would come to the door, doing up her hair, and call out, "Be patient, Ralph!"

It was time for the Albert Munson family to get things together and prepare to return to Asia. Grandpa Ralph was the professional packer. He would open the big steel steamer trunk and call for the family to bring the items to pack. Everything was wrapped in newspaper, tucked into nooks and corners. The delivery truck came and took the things away.

With Grandpa's prayer of blessings, they sailed for Singapore.

Ralph Waldo Munson was born on July 6, 1860 to Shubal and Electa Munson. He studied at Oberlin College and became the pioneer Adventist missionary to Indonesia.

Ralph Munson was pastor of this Pomona church in 1923.

Chapter 10

PIONEERS OF MANADO

The trip from California to Manado, Celebes, was very rough. Traveling on high seas, the deck was moving in all directions. Catherine got sick just watching the waves roll by the ship. If the weather was calm she would sit in a deck chair and knit socks or a sweater.

In all their travel the family experienced two typhoons, one cyclone and many tropical storms. These disturbances would last forty or fifty hours. Albert always took the responsibility of caring and entertaining the children. First, they visited the engine room of the ship, and the chief engineer showed them the great pistons going up and down that turned the huge steel shaft that drove the propeller. Then, they watched the firemen bend their sweaty backs to shovel coal into the roaring furnace that produced the superheated steam for the engine.

Another interesting event was visiting the captain's bridge. Here they were shown the compass and watched the sailor as he turned the great wheel which activated the rudder. While the captain was explaining the procedure, he stopped to give an order to the helmsman. He explained that he was correcting the direction of the ship. It was important that the sailor repeat each command as he obeyed and turned the wheel slightly.

Then they followed the ship's master into the chart room. Over the chart table there was a special map of the area in the ocean they were traveling. On the chart table was a similar map where the first mate (second in command) drew the course of the ship as he checked with instruments, like a sextant, to find their position on the map by reading the sun and using the chronometer (marine clock) to calculate the position of the ship on the charts.

When their family got back to the cabin, Albert emphasized the importance of obedience and spiritually knowing where one is in life. Albert asked the children, "What would happen if the sailor refused to follow the orders of the captain? The ship would get lost and might hit rocks and go down."

There were other excursions to take on board ship. On the big tourist liners they had gymnasiums, big swimming pools, and even playrooms for boys and girls. The inter-island steamers were exciting to the children because they stopped at small ports of many different islands. First the family would go ashore, take a local bus and see the town. If there was a church or Mission office in town they would visit those places. Missionaries' children may miss a lot of formal education but they gain a lot of social studies and geography, as well as biology. Sometimes their ship stopped at an Indonesian island port.

On one trip the family made, they heard a rumor that there was a python on board. They went to the rear of the ship and sitting on the deck was a large square box. As they headed for the box an islander warned them not to get too close, that there was a twenty-foot python inside, sleeping. They looked inside and saw the serpent's head with his eyes closed. Another time when the family was sailing from Sydney to Java, they saw a man holding a large bird with heavy legs. It was a young Australian emu. He could give a powerful kick with his heavy legs. Someone touched the bird's legs, and he kicked so hard the person was knocked off balance.

Usually the captain of the ship would tell the passengers when they would arrive at their destination. The next morning the children were up early, looking out the port hole to watch as the ship slowly entered the harbor of Manado. They passed an island called Manado Tua (Old Manado). It was an old extinct volcano. There were no wharf facilities, so they collected their baggage and carefully walked down the gangplank to board the launch waiting below them. Standing on the launch was their Chinese brother, Daniel Lim, waiting to help with the baggage to clear customs and immigration.

Arriving in Manado harbour in 1923, Albert led his wife and three small children down to the waiting boat rolling on the waves. One by one the sailors handed the children to the boat crew.

A Becha

The Albert Munson family in Manado

New mission home at Pal Dua, Manado

Their first view of the city of Manado was the ancient Portuguese fort overlooking the small shops and homes. It had massive walls, fourteen feet thick and guarded by ancient cannons. Small surreys drawn by ponies clattered down the narrow streets. The family hired a couple of "bechas" and rode off to their rental home on Sixth Street (called Batu Anam).

Father Albert settled the family in the home and arranged for a young girl to help care for sister Iva and do the housework. Albert helped with unpacking their goods, then he went to town to look for furniture and make application to work in Minehasa, the area controlled by the Dutch Colonial government.

He met the governor and was told he could not preach outside of the city of Manado, and that it would take some time for his permit to be granted. Also, he could not hold public meetings.

Undaunted, he discussed the problem with the small company of believers that had been raised by the colporteur, Daniel Lim. They suggested that the church could hold a corn-roast. Several people had been prepared for baptism by Brother Lim. They suggested that they invite people to come and have food for celebration and spiritual food for all.

The ladies brought their pots and pans and cooked a tasty feast for the guests. Many people came to the feast and ate piles of roasted corn and platters of yellow rice (rice colored with turmeric) and fried bananas. The public enjoyed the fellowship. Pastor Albert put up his prophecy chart and provided spiritual food. When the police came to inspect, the members took down the charts. Then they invited the police to enjoy the good food.

Finally, the governor gave Albert permission to preach and baptize. The local chief, Mr. Sumaiku, helped to introduce the church to the local authorities. Another influential man was Abner Laloan. He rented his home to Albert and Catherine and supported the church in many ways.

One of the first churches to be organized was in the town of Ratahan. It was the center of the agra-business of gathering cloves for the spice trade. Albert would visit this and many other villages like Tete, Tomohon, Tondano and Airmendidi and Kema. All these villages had interests and he would stay and prepare the people for accepting the Christian faith. As companies of believers sprang up he trained their leaders to follow Bible principles of action. He preached righteousness by faith, emphasizing the true Bible Sabbath. On Sabbath morning the coconut plantations rang with the sound of congregations praising the Lord with song. The Manadonese people are very musical. Albert introduced to them the Adventist song book, "Lagu Sion" (Songs of Zion), which his own father, Ralph W. Munson, had translated twenty years earlier. Local talent blossomed as they built rosewood marimbas to accompany soloists and choirs. Others had been trained in music and organized choirs in every church.

Camp meeting was a time of great spiritual blessing. Hundreds attended and each church sponsored its own choir. One church had four choirs---the deacons' choir, Dorcas ladies' choir, youth choir and the children's choir. With great rejoicing these dear members sang the praises of our Saviour.

In just six years the Holy Spirit moved on the hearts of over six hundred Manadonese to be baptized. The attitude of these believers was much appreciated. They insisted on building their own churches. Everybody helped in mixing cement, carrying lumber, setting doors and windows, nailing timbers on walls and roof. Today, beyond the campus of Mount Klabat University there is an Adventist church every two or three miles! Mount Klabat volcano is almost dormant but the real fire is in the youth of the church there.

Albert was motivated by the words of Jesus, "This gospel of the Kingdom shall be preached in all the world." The Spice Islands were within a day or two of travel by island ferries. When he visited the island of Ambon, he took his prophetic charts with him. He did not lie around on deck chairs to admire the scenery. He set up his chart wherever the passengers on the ferry were sitting and started to tell them stories from the Bible as illustrated by his art work. He shared the joy and hope of the gospel and the Second Coming of Jesus. Upon arriving at the island of Ambon, he announced that he planned to continue the Bible story session. He held his meetings in a private home. On one visit to this island he held a series of public meetings. The local ministers were not happy that he was preaching in public, so they decided to challenge him to public debate. He told them that all he had to do was ask them one question. "Show me in the Bible that God made Sunday a holy day." Many Ambonese Christians joined the Adventist church and this place became a strong missionary center.

While the family lived at Batu Anam house, Albert wanted to hire a gardener. One day a young man came from the Muslim area of Gorongtalo. He had been rejected by his family because he wanted to be a Christian, so he came to our Mission for help.

His name was Arsak Kadir. As he fled his home he hid in a large bush. Two villagers were chasing him, intending to do him harm. As they slashed the bush with their long knives they did not get him. That night he fled and was at the Mission office seeking help. Albert called the boy to his home and gave him a room in his house. George and Harold were delighted. Arsak showed them how to make kites. He also taught them how to play native games and prepare coconuts for the kitchen. A few months later Arsak trained to be a colporteur. He worked up to become a leader in the book sales program and stayed in this work for years.

It was at this home that the Lord gave the family a baby boy, born August 26, 1927. He was named Paul William Munson. The three children were happy to have a baby boy to play with. When Catherine came home from the hospital, the family stood around her bed to get a chance to hold the baby.

The Mission built a house for the family in Manado. It was nice to move into a brand-new house. No rats, no roaches, and it was easy to keep clean. The place was located out of town and Catherine was concerned about being alone with the children when Albert was visiting the outlying areas.

Before Albert left on his trip to the islands, they got a yellow puppy named Sammy. One night a drunk man came by singing loudly and shouting obscene language. He called the missionaries mosquitoes, sucking the blood of the Indonesians. Catherine was worried, so she bolted all doors and windows and sent Sammy out the front door. The man was having a hard time staggering up the front steps to the house. Sammy rushed down the steps, barking loudly. The fellow hesitated at the first landing, cursed the dog and lunged up the steps. That did it. Sammy grabbed the man's pant leg and pulled hard. The man turned in fear and stumbled down to the road and staggered away. Sammy got a special treat that night.

Albert and Katie were concerned that their children had no playmates The older children were fantasizing a lot, inventing "play language" and talking to imaginary friends. Iva was talking to her make-believe "Betty Butterfly."

Instead of buying a lot of toys, Albert went to a friend who was an auto salesman and asked for one of the boxes used for transporting Morris cars from England to Indonesia. He told his friend that it was for the children. The box was delivered and Albert got out his tools and transformed it into a playhouse by cutting out windows and a door. The children spent hours in that place as they continued to chatter in play language.

Another concern that bothered the parents was the lack of a formal education in the English language. They needed to learn to read, so they hired an intelligent young man named Martin Laloan who spoke English.

George and his siblings liked Martin. He told them funny stories and taught them local ballads. Albert checked up on their reading skills. If Harold or George made a reading mistake, their ears were twisted or pulled. "Ouch."

The children loved it when their parents planned picnics to places like Lake Tondano or Airmendidi Hot Springs. They also liked to play with the Pandelaki children who lived beside beautiful Lake Tondano. It was an interesting place. It was a crater of an old volcano. There was still activity in the crater. It had filled up with water and once in a while the water in the lake moved as the crater experienced an earthquake. The fishermen who were catching fish would pull in their nets and head for home when the water started to jump.

The children will never forget the big earthquake that took place one noon time. Their house had two stories. The family had just gathered around the dining table for lunch. Dad Albert had not arrived so the family sat down and offered grace. Suddenly the water glasses started to dance and water was spilling out. The light was swinging wildly. Suddenly there was a crash as the book case emptied out onto the floor. Catherine grabbed Paul and they all headed for the front door and outside. Just as they crossed the threshold, the front steps broke away from the house, leaving a four-inch gap! They all stumbled down the stairs as the earth rolled like ocean waves. George fell down on the gravel driveway and started crying. He shouted, "Mother, is this the end of the world?"

Of course Catherine calmed the family as they stood holding on to her skirts and waiting for things to calm down. There was an empty field next door, and they could see a four-inch-wide crack in the earth running across the field. As they stood there stunned, they heard Albert laughing as he pushed his bike along the road. He told the family that he was riding his bike when the earthquake struck and the road started to crack. The road rose up like waves, and he could not ride his bike. Every time he tried to ride, he fell off! So he had to push the bike home.

That evening Albert gathered his family and explained that Jesus had warned us about earthquakes in the last days. There would be many earthquakes, but the end was not yet. We must be ready. The children have never forgotten the spiritual lessons learned from morning and evening worship and singing of hymns.

It was time for the family to go on furlough. One of Albert's last duties was to hold an anointing and baptism service for a very ill brother. He was a leper and the disease had left his body badly disfigured.

Albert took George along that day. They walked to a village by the ocean. The members showed them the little grass hut where they found the poor man lying on a grass mat. Eleven-year-old George could hardly believe his eyes when they stepped into the dark hut. There lay an emaciated body, limbs bent and lying in a fetal position, fingerless hands, and legs but no feet! The stench was hard to endure. A big hole in his face for a mouth and empty eye sockets, no ears and great lumps all over his body.

Tears flowed down their eyes as Albert talked quietly with trembling voice. "My dear brother, do you love Jesus? Do you want Him to heal you of your sins and your diseases?" They could not understand the sounds that came out of his mouth, but they knew what he meant when he shook his head affirmatively. Albert took out his little flask of anointing oil and then pleaded with the Great Physician to heal this poor brother as he poured a little oil on his hairless head. Then tenderly Albert picked up the sixty pounds of humanity, stood up and walked slowly towards the ocean side. A few believers followed to the water. They began to sing, "Just as I am without one plea, but that Thy blood was shed for me, and that Thou bid'st me come to Thee, Oh, Lamb of God, I come, I come."

Albert stood at the edge of the ocean water and said, "Today, it is my desire that the Lord, if it is His will, may cleanse our brother of his sins and heal his diseased body." Then he prayed in the name of the Father, His Son Jesus, and the Holy Spirit, Amen. He walked into the waves and slowly immersed the dear soul into the gently lapping waves.

This was Albert's last baptism in Manado. The family left for their furlough in 1929. Five years later they received a letter stating that the Lord had arrested the brother's disease and that he went to sleep in Jesus and awaits that wonderful day of resurrection when he will receive a new body!

Chapter 11

SNAKES IN SINGAPORE

It was the summer of 1930 that the Munson family arrived in Singapore. The name of the city in the Malay language means "Lion Harbor," in modern terms the harbor where the British Lion stays. Even in the Thirties the island of Singapore was a military base of the Royal Army and Royal Navy of Great Britain.

However, there were still strips of jungle with cobras and pythons and other creatures of the forest. Down in the center of the city were the Botanical Gardens with monkeys and other animals running loose.

The Malayian Union Mission compound was at 399 Upper Serangoon road, just three blocks from a strip of jungle. They lived out of town and all missionaries' children were warned not to go barefoot and watch out for snakes.

One day Harold was running in the tall grass beside Eric Johanson's house. He heard a hissing sound and stopped. Sure enough, there was a cobra with his head puffed out, ready to strike. They called the gardener and with one swipe of his grass-cutting sickle the snake was dead.

The children enjoyed playing with the other Mission youth. At one time there were fourteen children of Mission families. They also liked to associate with the children of Chinese and Malay and Indian families. They went swimming together at Mt. Emille swimming pool or at Katong beach. On some occasions they had picnics at Poongal, the Mission rest home.

On Sabbaths their parents took them to visit the Japanese garden behind Pidadary Cemetery or to feed the monkeys at the Botanical Gardens.

School in Singapore was a real challenge! Not only did the Munson children have a weakness in reading but they had no training in math. The Mission School in

Singapore was based on the British standard system. It was called a spiral system of learning. The teachers began algebra in the fourth standard. George was in this class and he had no idea what they were talking about when the teacher said x plus y equals 10. He was in a corner. The class was made up of smart Chinese boys, some Indians and some Malays. He was the only white boy in the class. They were studying English history and learning the King's English. George was the dumbest kid in the room. Wow! What a handicap. Harold was having a hard time also, but he just cut up and drew cartoons all day. Iva was getting the basics so she was getting a better foundation.

They had another challenge to meet on the playground at recess time. Since they looked different, the boys called them "Angmokao," a local word meaning red- nosed foreign devil. They had already faced this in Manado and understood what their parents had advised. Since rubber was very cheap, the kids could buy a bag of rubber bands for a few pennies. For some reason it was fun to wage rubber band war! They divided into groups and sometimes tempers would flare and feelings as well as legs were hurt. One day, after a hot clash of "rubber band war," an Indian boy tripped George as he returned to the classroom. They got into a tussle and his head smashed into the brick pillar. George was not going to cry in front of dozens of Asian kids. He staggered home and cried to his mother, saying he did not want to go to school.

Harold had been punished that day for fighting. So Catherine took both boys down to the principal's office. Well, the result was harder to take than being bullied by Asian kids. Their parents were being moved to Sarawak, Borneo. They enrolled the boys in the Home Study Institute. They did not realize that the correspondence course would be quite difficult. The mail system at that time would be very slow taking sometimes three months to get to Washington and back to Sarawak. The last stretch of the trip would be held up, since the ship came to Kuching once a month. Albert made arrangements with the local school to have the boys supervised by a local teacher who knew English and could explain the lessons. Then Albert planned his work so that he could take

Malaysian Signs Press, Singapore.
Malaysian Mission Headquarters

them out with him into the jungle for special experiences. He also went to the local library and borrowed books for them to read. They were glad that their father found ways to keep them occupied.

Back in Singapore, Albert was asked in 1930 or 1931 to be acting chairman of the Mission committee while Elder J. G. Gjording and family were on furlough. For years he had only a bike for transportation. Since his duties were heavier he needed a car. But the price was high. He decided to buy a used car. It was an Italian Fiat touring model. He had no experience in buying cars, and this one turned out to be a "lemon." He hired a young man to repair the car, but he turned out to be a fake. So he was left with a broken-down car and was still riding the famous "mosquito buses" (a Ford Model T built with seats for eight people).

The financial crash of the Great Depression in 1929 caused many headaches for all mission fields, and Malaysian Union was no exception. The Mission president, Elder G. J. Gjording was on furlough. Albert Munson was asked to be acting president. Elder E. J. Johanson, a missionary from Australia, was treasurer of the Union. The Far Eastern Division gave the Union its appropriation but it was cut so that the treasurer worked for hours but could not produce a balanced budget, so he asked Albert to call a special meeting of the mission staff. They had to make some serious decisions. They spent hours trying to decide whether to send missionaries home or cut the salaries. What to do? The meeting ran into the wee hours of the night. The treasurer told the committee that they would have to cut the salaries forty per cent. The missionaries did not want to go home, so the only option was to make ten per cent cuts each year for four years. Tension was high. Albert finally pulled out a blank sheet of paper and drew a cartoon. He showed himself in four panels. First he was fully dressed and standing on a box. The treasurer was standing in front with a big pair of shears. He told Albert this is not going to hurt. On panel two, marked ten per cent, Albert's pants and coat as well as his hat had been heavily trimmed. Panel three showed the result of severe trimming. The last panel showed Albert wearing a "G" string. He was looking at the top of a coconut tree and a monkey was beckoning to him to join him among the coconuts. The cartoon was passed around and everyone had a hearty laugh. The decision was made to make four ten-per-cent cuts to be spread out over four years.

While the family was still in Singapore, the children experienced a very special spiritual event. Elder Meade McGuire was sent by the church to hold revival services in the schools and churches of the Far East. The school asked Elder McGuire to hold a week of prayer service. His sermons were good and since the school taught English, the chapel was full with all the pupils present for the meetings.

He was a man of God and a friend of the boys and girls. Many children responded to the pastor's appeals. Several of their fellow classmates joined the baptismal class. The baptism was held at Poongal in the ocean beside the rest home. Twenty-two young people were baptized that day which included Carlton Gjording, George Munson, Madeline and Pauline Bunch, Naomi and Betty Bowers. Elder Gjording, the Mission president, baptized the group. It was September 12, 1932.

Chapter 12

MIRACLES IN SARAWAK

In 1931, the Mission committee assigned Elder Gus Youngberg to pioneer the work of God in the northern part of the State of Sarawak. The acting Union Mission president, Elder Fordyce Detamore and Albert Munson had been helping him choose the right piece of property. Since land costs in Bentulu were too high and more than the Mission could pay, they decided to go south of Bentulu and purchase a piece of property on the Tatau river.

After the Mission leaders had returned to Singapore, Gus headed for the Tatau property. He wanted to get housing ready for his family's arrival. He arranged for local workers to help him in his building project. Gus knew he had to get some means of transportation for hauling building supplies and doing mission travel. Two Mission leaders sailed to Kuching in South Sarawak and searched for a good boat that would speed up the program on the Tatau river. Finally they found a twenty-four-foot cabin cruiser that would not cost more than $600.00. The boat was just right for the mission work, making it possible to travel upstream for one hundred miles.

Earlier, Gus had drawn sketches and plot plans for the Union committee to look at. All buildings were authorized. The property had one hundred acres of land and sixty would be suitable for rice cultivation. Gus erected the houses on a hill which they later called Bukit Nyala.

When Norma, his wife, and children arrived they were delighted to be together again. Being a good missionary, she promptly set up a home school for her four school-aged children. Native men helped Gus Youngberg with the building program. Everybody was warned about the black Malaysian cobra. The children wanted to go barefoot, but they were warned. Elder and Mrs. Youngberg were given help by national missionary workers like Elder Sinaga, whose home island was northern Sumatra. During the building process Brother Sinaga had located in the village of Sidang so that he could learn the language and study the culture of the people. Later he would be a help as Elder Youngberg joined him to work together for the people in the Tatau district.

Just as soon as the clinic building was completed and the people learned that they could get medical help, the Mission became a busy place.

Albert and Catherine Munson were assigned to work in south Sarawak, with headquarters in Kuching, the capital city of the state. This town was also the center of the Rajah's government. The Rajah was Sir Viner Brooke, cousin of the original Rajah Sir James Brooke. Albert was assigned to work among the Sea Dyaks who lived along the Sadong river. The territory was called Serian.

After visiting Kuching and looking for a house to rent, Albert returned to Singapore to get his family. The household goods were packed for shipment to Sarawak. Then the family had to find transportation to the dock and take a small launch to the ship anchored in the harbor. The small ship was named "Rajah Brooke" after the White Rajah.

Following the usual pattern of mission travel, the family found their cabins and then set out to explore the ship and watch the final loading of the vessel. It was a freighter and passenger ship, bringing mail once a month to Borneo. The children watched the sailors raise the anchor as the signals from the bridge rang out for the engineers to turn on the steam and start the engine. The trip took just a couple of days.

On the morning of the third day the children heard the engines slow down so everybody headed for the top deck. The ship was entering the Kuching River. The captain was very cautious as he crossed the usual sandbar at the mouth of the river Albert suggested that the family move over to the starboard side of the ship. On the shore of the river on the hill stood an old Buddhist temple. It was built by early Chinese traders who visited the islands to sell large earthen jars and brass gongs to the native shaman priests, who used them in their rituals. The temple was built not long after the Sung

Wars. Many refugees from that war left China in small boats and drifted to Borneo.

The ship steamed up the river for a couple of hours; then the river made a turn and they could see the city. To the right of the river was the Palace of the Rajah and an ancient eighteenth century fort mounted with 40-pound cannons. Over the fort flew the Union Jack and the Flag of the Kingdom of Sarawak.

The ship slowed down as small sampans scurried across the water, and native schooners loaded freight along the docks of the bund. Albert said, "Listen," as the ship sounded its horn and then suddenly an answering boom came from the fort as soldiers fired the old eighteenth century cannon. The cannons are fired every day at noon and once a month when the ship comes in with mail from Singapore. As the family looked out over the city, they saw people coming from all directions. The mail was in and just as soon as the ship was secured the mail bags were unloaded. People stood in line waiting for the post office to distribute the mail.

With exclamations of wonder, the Munson family went to their cabins and picked up their baggage. As soon as they were through with the customs and immigration officers, they hired a taxi and were off up the hill to their future home.

For a few weeks the family would live in an old brick mansion. Their first night in Kuching was scary to the kids. They had a light supper and everybody washed their feet for bed. George and Harold were led into a huge bedroom with rattling shutters. Their Mom tucked them in bed after they said their prayers, and when the lights were turned off it became spooky. The place smelled old and moldy. Iva and Paul slept in smaller beds in the master bedroom with their parents. It had been a big day and all drifted off to sleep. Suddenly at nine o'clock they woke up to the loud calls of the night watchman. They did not know this and called their Mother. She came in and told them that each house has a watchman and at nine, midnight and three o'clock he calls out the time. "Pookul sembilang," he called out, meaning (in the Malay language) "Nine o'clock." In the morning the children inspected the old house It was like Harry Potter's haunted castles. As night came on, thousands of jungle insects sounded off like a band and what a chorus!

When the packing crates were opened, the children scrambled for their bikes. The older boys had fun exploring the community. Albert wrestled with the furniture into the rental home just across the road. He walked the three miles up Serian road to arrange for the boys to study at Sunnyhill School. George studied his correspondence lessons in an adjacent classroom while Harold sat in the teacher's class--- both supervised by teacher Choo Sing Fat.

Every morning before eight o'clock the boys got ready for school and started to pedal down the road past a Catholic Boys school. A group of local boys spied the white boys and began taunting them, daring those long-nosed, yellow-haired white boys by blocking their way with a long ominous line of school boys, They saw what was coming so they made a quick plan to divert around by passing up the bank of the road. The trick worked once. But a crisis came when the road was totally blocked and the Munson boys were harassed. So Dad Albert went to the priest and quickly settled the problem.

Missionary parents have many concerns for their children. Growing up in Asia is not like being brought up in rural California or urban Los Angeles. It is expected that Christian children cannot retaliate and must model a higher standard of behavior. However, they enjoyed learning local children' s games, making and flying their own kites. They also loved to attend feasts. They were fond of some ethnic foods and hated others. Their parents arranged for national children to attend their birthday parties and take part in picnics.

Albert often took the older boys on trips into the jungle to whet our interest in mission service. They took an active part in service and helped their father, and it was a welcome change from writing lessons and reading.

Elder J. T. Pohan and his wife from Sumatra provided strong leadership in establishing the new school planned for the Sea Dyaks of Serian. Brother and Sister Pauner came to teach. Both couples had finished their school work at the Malayan Seminary in Singapore.

Dad decided he needed George's help to clear the jungle and build a dormitory for the new school at Serian. He decided to call the school "Ayer Manis School," meaning "Sweet

The Albert Munson family in Kuching

The Sunnyhill Adventist School, located three miles out of Kuching, the capitol of the state of Sarawak.

In 1933, Albert, with Pastor Pohan and teacher Chu Sing fat, pose with George and a group of Dayak villagers.

Water." He chose this name because there was a spring of sweet water on the property. The spring was high up on the mountain behind the property. They got out their bags and packed mosquito nets and work clothes, and George asked Dad to buy him a parang (work knife used by the natives). Mother protested (she was afraid he would cut himself.). George promised to be very careful.

When all was ready, Dad and George grabbed their bags and headed for the bus station downtown. The bus was very crowded—chickens under the long benches, pigs in bamboo pokes on the bus roof, rice bags and smelly dried fish in big bundles piled high. As they stepped into the bus it started to rain. Albert mumbled under his breath, "It's going to be a long, hard day." All went well until they left the paved highway and started driving on the dirt road. The rain increased and soon the bus driver was losing traction and bogging down in the red mud of the road. In no time the bus slid off the road and lurched to a stop. The driver ordered everybody out to help push the old crate. After some effort they got the bus back on the road. Sweaty, mud-splattered passengers crawled back onto the hard benches. The native men lit up their clove-laced cigarettes and the ladies took another cud of siri (beetle nut and henna leaf, a wild narcotic that smelled like foul drain cleaner). Albert winked at me as he wrinkled up his nose at the smell of naked, sweaty bodies, gross! They slid off the road several times that day, finally arriving at the thirty-seventh mile post where the school property was located. Brother Pohan was calmly waiting for them under a banana leaf to keep the rain off his head.

As they climbed off the bus, happy to leave the squawking chickens, squealing pigs, the two white people surprised the local passengers by getting off at such a wild, forsaken place. Brother Pohan welcomed them to Ayer Manis Mission, pointing to an old thatched hut up on the hill, announcing, "Welcome to Serian Hotel." After a good laugh he added, "And when you gentlemen are ready, there's your bath and shower," (pointing to the little jungle stream and pool just across the road).

The thatched hut where we stayed had been used by government road builders. It was a dining cabin with a kitchen in back. Dad and George decided to use one of the tables for a bed, put their sheets down, and tied up the mosquito nets. Mom had prepared a basket of rice balls and other goodies for lunches. They were tired and after a refreshing bath, they slept well, even on the hard table boards. The next morning at sun-up, the jungle was alive with bird calls from hundreds of feathered throats. Dad and George heard the sound of axes and parangs and were eager to join the men already clearing the jungle just a short walk away. They had already felled most of the trees on the three-acre plot. George joined the natives, pulled out his new parang and started to lop off limbs of the trees that had been felled the day before by the hired villagers. Following local customs, they left the felled trees on the ground until the leaves dried in the hot sun, then they set fire to the dead foliage, which burned as far as the green jungle. The logs were then milled into boards for the building project.

Dad and Julious Pohan discussed the building plans that Pohan had drawn. There was to be a wooden cottage of about six hundred square feet made of logs and pole construction. Locally sawn boards made up the floor with split bamboo for the walls. In those days they used kerosene lamps for light and cooked on fire pits in the kitchen. Julious Pohan and his wife were to live in the cottage with the large front porch to be used as the classroom. A dormitory for about twelve village boys was constructed behind this building.

Outside, next to the boys dorm, a barrel was sunk in the ground to store water from the fresh water spring high up on the mountain. The supply pipeline was made by inserting the small end of a bamboo pole into the large end of another pole, supported above ground by sapling uprights. All material for this project came from the property. From the barrel of water the men dug a ditch past the house down to a large pool where the Pohans planned to grow kangkong and watercress and also raise fish in the pond.

One day George was helping dig this channel when an older village lady and her teenage daughter came to talk to Albert. After an awkward eternity, Dad called him over. Chuckling to himself, Dad said, "This lady has come to sell her daughter so that you can have a wife and she will cook for us." Leaving Dad to enjoy the moment, George remembers his cheeks turning hot with embarrassment and walking away mumbling, "No way, no way."

Working hard all day, by nightfall they were covered with black soot and caked with sweat. They walked back to the cabin, grabbed their towels, soap and dry clothes and headed for their "Borneo Spa." Leaving their dirty clothes on the creek bank, they waded "skinny-dipping" into the water to wash up. Soon Albert let out a yelp, "Look what we have?" George looked up, thinking there was a snake in the pool. Albert was staring up on the roadside bank. There, lined up like swallows on a telephone line, was a row of curious village women and their daughters, taking in the strange sight as if it was Hollywood "blockbuster!" Albert turned and ran up the bank yelling like a wild Indian. Talk about a wild "scatteration." The crowd scattered like a flock of startled hens!

It was Harold's turn to go along with Dad and George on our next mission trip. This time they were going to Ingather at ten Chinese gold mines. Dad suggested they pack a good lunch and bring along their bicycles. This would be a good lesson in applied chemistry.

They rode to the riverside and hired an outboard-powered sampan. The boys loaded their bikes on the front deck of the prau and sat on the floor under the canopy. A few miles up river they tied up to a wharf, got their bikes off and rode to the gold mines of Bao, formerly an old British mine. Fifty years earlier they had run out of gold veins, so the Chinese businessmen wrote a contract to extract the gold from the tailings left by the former miners. In the 1930s, ten Chinese contractors were working the tailings and finding new veins of ore.

On the way the boys were hot, so they stopped at a small lake that had been formed when the huge British steam shovels dug the ore from the ground. The water was inviting so they peeled off and had a swim. After eating their lunch with gusto, they got back on their bikes. It did not take long until they were standing in the office of the head gold miner, a fine Chinese gentleman who welcomed them to his company. He showed them how the rock was broken up in big crushers

Albert took his sons, George and Harold, to visit the Bao gold mines to request donations for his village school project.

and the ore poured into big cement vats. A solution of cyanide was run into the vats. After soaking for the right length of time, the cyanide acid renders the gold in the solution. That liquid is run into a smaller vat containing zinc. This black muddy substance is poured into the smelter and the furnace fire is turned on.

While they waited for the furnace to do its work, they went into the manager's office. Dad talked to him about our mission schools in Kuching and the new project for the Sea Dyaks. He asked for a donation to help in these school projects. The kind gentleman donated $100.00. Dad thanked him profusely. The manager also wrote a note to the other mine operators suggesting a donation. That day Dad collected $900.00 from the miners. Before they left, the manager wanted to show the boys something. He went into a side room and came out holding something behind his back. He asked them to close their eyes and hold out their hands. When they opened their eyes again, they held $14,000.00 worth of gold bars in each hand. He told them this was almost pure gold. Then he invited the boys to follow him to see what was inside the furnace. At first all they saw was a black scum, but as he skimmed off the black dross on the surface, the molten gold shone like a mirror! This reminded them of the description in the Bible of the refiner's fire producing pure character.

My Dad was getting very concerned about Mom's health—she had to spend much time in bed. One day she called George to her bedside. She wanted to teach him how to bake the weekly batch of bread. The kitchen helper did not know how. First he was to prepare the potato yeast so that the batch of bread dough would rise, ready for baking. George took notes by Mother's bedside. To get good flour for the bread, Dad took him down to buy a few pounds of hard wheat from the Indian miller. At home he carefully washed the wheat and dried it in the sun and then carried the cleaned wheat back to the miller to make sure he did not grind it in the same machine used for chili peppers.

Next George fired up the two charcoal pots and set the sheet metal oven over them. In a large bowl he mixed together the right amounts of bread ingredients and added the flour slowly. When it was too stiff to stir he turned the dough out on a flour-covered surface and kneaded in the remaining flour, then set it aside to rise.

After the dough was ready, it was molded into loaves and put into oiled pans. While the loaves were rising, George got out the rolling pin and rolled out the remaining dough, spread butter on it and sprinkled a mixture of cinnamon and sugar over it. After making a roll of the dough, he cut off two-inch sections, put them on an oiled pan and set them aside to rise. Sometimes the bread was too hard and even the family dogs (Bala and Nigger) could not eat it. His first bread was nothing like Mother's delicious loaves, but with practice he learned to do it right.

Mother Katie's condition grew worse. She had been hemorrhaging when the ambulance came to take her to the hospital, and the children were sad and worried. Before Mom left, Dad gathered them around Mother and prayed with the family earnestly, asking the Lord to have mercy on his wife. As the ambulance pulled away with Dad and a very sick wife, he asked George and his somber siblings to pray for our mother. It was Christmas time, but their thoughts were far from the usual Yuletide excitement. George was over fifteen, Harold was fourteen, Iva was twelve and Paul was seven. The "amah" cooked rice and vegetables, but they were not hungry. In those days there were no telephones for missionaries and no radio.

Finally after the most terrifying night vigil, Dad came home to his worried little family. "How's Mommy? Is she going to be O.K.?" The doctor had worked all day on her, but to no avail. That night they went to bed after a prayer session with Dad. The next morning he left the children solemn, with the younger ones crying.

Christmas Day was a critical time for Katie and her dear little family. The lady doctor, sensing nothing more could be done, so she hung up her stethoscope and went home to her Christmas party. Dad was furious at this callous disregard, so he stayed by her side all night. He could see she was losing her strength rapidly, so he told Katie that he was going to an empty room to pray.

With tears of grief, Dad reminded the Lord that his children needed their Mother and that he wanted to stay in Borneo and share the love of Jesus with souls lost in sin. He pleaded for the healing power of Jesus. When he finished praying, he went back to her room. As he entered he felt there was a change. She asked him, "Did you see the person, dressed in white, leave the room?" "No," he whispered. "That person in white stood by my bed and touched me. I felt a power run all through my body. I feel so much better now!" What a gift? Christmas, since that time, has been a memorial of that wonderful miracle.

Medical professionals and the Mission leaders advised Albert to return with his family to California. On their way home the family stopped in Singapore so that Catherine could gain strength for the journey. The Italian liner, "S.S. Conti Rosso" would bring them back to their Motherland.

As they boarded, the children waved goodbye to their playmates. Remaining dockside a few moments longer, George asked, Naomi Bowers, "Please write?" She replied, "You write first." He did just that and mailed it from Hawaii. It was the beginning of a friendship that culminated in marriage six years later, in 1940. They are still pals after sixty-five years.

The family transferred at the bustling port of Hong Kong to a "President" liner to finish the journey to Los Angeles, California. After major surgery at White Memorial Hospital, Catherine regained her health--for 40 more years--outliving Albert by one year.

Indeed, God performed many miracles in Sarawak. The witness of the Tan family as they pioneered in Kuching, the gift of free land for the Ayer Manis School, Catherine's miraculous healing—all resulted in the marvelous Providential growth of the Lord's work. Today, in 2006, fourteen thousand believers worship in eighty churches in Sarawak, waiting for the coming of the Lord.

Chapter 13

LIVING IN DESERT HEAT

The Munson family arrived from Singapore in 1934 to face the dry summer of Southern California, a one-hundred-ten degree heat wave! The kids had never been so hot in their lives! The dry heat of this desert-like climate was burning then up. They filled the bathtub in the tiny bathroom and took turns crawling in to cool off. Poor Mom was drained and sweating in the kitchen ironing clothes and baking a roast in the gas oven! Dad was in Glendale arranging for a pastoral job with the local Conference leaders. Mother was recovering from major surgery and helping the family settle in a little adobe-styled house on Carmen Street in La Sierra. The elementary school was at the end of the road on Sierra Vista Street. Melvin Munson's family lived across the road from the school in a small, one-acre ranch where Aunt Harriet kept fifteen hundred chickens, one goat and a milk cow. Albert's family got eggs and milk from Harriet's farm. We children spent countless hours working and playing with our cousins.

Each member of the family fit into the lifestyle of Riverside county that summer. Harold and I were excited about the local boys riding their bikes around the roads of the College campus. One road was right in front of our house, and it was steep. This road was eroded by many winter rains and was deeply rutted. Albert had just purchased a family car, an old 1929 Chevy, so we boys did not beg for bicycles. Our cousins suggested we check out the local junk yard. Dad took us down and sure enough, we found an old bike frame with no seat or tires and paid just one dollar for it! With a couple of secondhand tires, an old seat and some red paint, we had our bike.

A creative kid built a neat soapbox racer. That did it! Everyone had to do the same. So back to the venerable junk yard. In no time there was a whole squadron of racers. Every style that a kid's imagination could create---decorated in every color of paint found in the garage paint box.

One day I took my humble racer to the top of the hill and started down the track. Part way down, as I gained speed, I hit a big rut and hurtled into space. When I hit the ground my racer was gone and I landed right on my spine! A constant reminder of my "parachute" jump off Grandpa Innes' barn in Australia.

Too soon summer was over and it was time to register for school. Also, I was hoping I could be accepted into the academy as a freshman. When the registrar checked my record of the Home Study Institute, we were told the records were not complete. At sixteen years of age, I was doomed to take eighth grade over again! We went down to the elementary school to join the long line to register. Head and shoulders taller than the other boys, I was devastated. When we got back to the car the tears flowed! My Father was a compassionate parent. When I got home Mother shared with me her day of disappointment: "After finishing at Avondale College, I applied at Sydney Sanitarium for the nurses course. The examining physician turned me down because my little finger was missing on my right hand! It was hard to take. But I took courage and applied at Sydney City College. The examiner was an Ob-Gyn physician. During the interview, I cautiously shared that there was something I must tell him. Shyly I told him of my deformed hand. He responded by holding up his own right hand. He had the same missing finger! He told me that if I fulfilled my desire to be a midwife, I might save a baby's life by using that smaller hand in certain difficult birth procedures."

After that I did not feel so bad. The first day of school I met another boy, Clayton Roderick, from Lake Elsinore, who was also sixteen years old. We became friends and liked to work together on community projects. One day we got out our shovels and carved out a switchback trail all the way to Two-Bits Rock at the summit of the hill behind the College.

I enjoyed raising Bantam chickens, starting with a little hen, then I got a pretty little rooster. He had a beautiful tail and was a cocky little fellow. When the school sponsored a pet parade, I built a little wagon, decorated it with lots of bright red and gold paint. I made a harness for the rooster and hitched him to the cart. High up on the wagon was a sign advertising the College. (Four gold and crimson letters—S.C.J.C.—Southern California Junior College.) During the parade the other animals were obeying well but young Banty tried his best to get rid of the harness and wagon. I had to push the bird along, "Banty" complained all the way! But we walked off with first prize!

In winter, my parents took us to play in the snow on Mount Baldy; in the spring to see the great display of desert flowers. We saw the landscape painted orange and purple with California poppies and lupines.

My Father was assigned to be pastor of the Eagle Rock Seventh-day Adventist church. Our family moved to Stanley Street in Glendale to be close to the Glendale Union Academy where the children would be attending elementary school and the Academy.

With three children attending school, the family was facing financial stress. One day Dad took me aside, suggested I find a summer job so that I could help with the family finances. My Uncle Paul was an experienced house painter working for Ed Rogers, who had a paint crew of over forty men. Paul helped me get a job as a painter's helper for twenty-five cents per hour. It was very rewarding for me to bring home a check to Mother so that the family could have funds for tuition money and food.

Following the advice of my parents, I signed up to study printing at the Academy Press. This experience was good, for I could help earn my own tuition as well as gain experience for my future career. Dad also advised me to try to finish my academy studies in three years, so I signed up to take geometry night classes at the Glendale High School. (These experiences helped me later in mission service.)

As you can see Academy was a very busy time for me after hours—with printing at the Press and working with the paint crew on Sundays and summer vacations. I was happy to keep busy, for there were many temptations in the city life of Los Angeles.

At Glendale Academy, I became interested in learning to play the trombone. At a Sears store I bought one and an instruction book that included a self-help section. After some coaching from my boss, Ed Rogers, I joined the Academy band. My brother Harold learned to play clarinet and played in the Lynwood Academy band. Later, I played in the Pacific Union College band.

The social life at the Academy was puzzling to me. The girls hoped that the boys would ask for a date and take them out to the Saturday night entertainment. If they asked the same girl every time they could say they were steady dates. I did not agree with this philosophy but instead had many friends among the girls at the school. I took out different girls each Saturday evening, which puzzled my classmates. One day, in English class, I was sitting low in my chair when someone behind me slipped out my wallet and found a picture of Naomi Bowers. They passed it around, but no one knew the mystery girl. When they returned the picture, they demanded, "Who is this good-looking girl?" I told them: "You'll find out soon enough." Since 1934 I had been corresponding with Naomi who was attending Far Eastern Academy located in Shanghai, China.

In 1937, Naomi's family had returned on furlough to New England to visit family members there. After furlough, Naomi would attend college in America, and her sister Betty would return to finish academy in Shanghai.

Before returning to Asia, the Bowers visited missionary friends in Glendale, California. I had looked forward to this visit with anticipation. Not only would I get better acquainted with Naomi and her family but she could meet my family again. Best of all, I could now show my classmates my "steady (mystery) girl."

One evening I escorted her to Elder Philip Knox's evangelistic meeting being held in a large tent in Glendale. When Naomi and I walked into the tent, all students, sitting on the last row of seats, did a quick "eyes right." Now they knew.

The Lyman Bowers family, on furlough in 1937

Albert Munson Family in Glendale
Back row: Harold, Paul, George; Front row: Iva, Catherine, Albert

Before Naomi arrived, I had purchased an old 1928 Model A Ford. I was proud to drive my "Singapore Girl" down Chevy Chase boulevard in my first car!

In 1937 I was earning enough to pay my own tuition plus help Harold and Iva with their school bills. My Uncle Paul had taken time to teach me how to paint carefully and keep things clean. My friend Roger Warner, an older student, needed someone to help in his landscaping jobs, so I joined him working in the yards of rich people in Glendale and Altadena. We worked in the homes of many Jewish families. It was fascinating to observe the lifestyles and rituals of these devout people.

I was unable to graduate with my class of 1938 but had made some wonderful friends. The teachers in the school had a strong spiritual impact on my life. Miss Katherine Speh, German and English teacher, was a spiritual mentor to the students. Mr. Jackson and Elder McCully were strong leaders in the Academy. All this was a help, pointing me forward to face college life, at Pacific Union College.

Chapter 14

DESERT CRISIS

In the spring of 1938, I was planning to register at Pacific Union College, located in Napa Valley in Northern California. This is the school my father had attended and nearly everyone had recommended. I knew I needed cash to register. With over one hundred dollars credit at the Academy, I went to the school treasurer to request a transfer of the funds to the College. I was told that since my siblings owed a debt to the school, my credit must be applied to the "family account."

I wrote to the College, stating that I needed to work at the College Press in the summer in order to build up a credit for the new school year. George Jeys, manager of the Press in Angwin, kindly allowed me to begin work right away. With this great break, I was able to register for the fall semester.

Naomi arranged to work at St. Helena Sanitarium dining room as a waitress and also to help bring patients in for hydrotherapy treatments. We saw each other about once a week. I arranged for rides down the hill to the Sanitarium or just hitchhiked my way. Once or twice during the summer I walked the whole six miles.

That first year of college was filled with studies, work at the Press and other extracurricular activities. Freshmen did not have visiting rights, so Naomi and I cherished every opportunity to meet at the dinner table or a quick greeting in the hall between classes. Later we were invited to have an early-morning breakfast at the popular lookout point, or other social events.

In those days, most students earned their tuition, board and room by working in some industrial department of the school. The College founders believed in the work-study principle outlined by the church founder, Ellen G. White. These work opportunities were basically the College Press, the book bindery, agriculture department along with poultry and dairy. Men and women could work in the offices or custodial agencies. Some of the huskier boys worked in the woods to fell trees and split firewood for the steam boilers. It was not easy to earn board and room with the economy just pulling out of the Great Depression. We survived on inexpensive food. Very few students had cars, but we would all jump into one car and head for Nabisco Company's Bay Area plant in Emeryville. We bought broken shredded wheat biscuits in gunny sacks for fifty cents. For breakfast we choked this down with a half pint of milk. Oh, how we pinched the pennies!

Like most mothers, my Mother would send me an extra five dollars to buy Navy surplus shoes. We students did not grumble about our poverty but just considered it a reality of life. Many students were planning to be missionaries; this taught us to be adaptable.

Part of the ministerial training given in those days was to gain experience for at least three months of training in selling religious books door to door as colporteurs. In the spring of 1939, I got acquainted with Oliver Jacques, a great-grandson of Ellen G White. We both decided to join the group planning to sell books in eastern Utah. Elder A. J. Werner, Publishing Secretary of the Pacific Union, came to the College to recruit students and train them for this program.

Oliver and I were assigned the territory in Deuchene county, stretching from Heber City, near Salt Lake City, all the way down Highway 40 to Vernal, Utah, on the border of Colorado. Before we left we spent several hours learning our canvasses and getting instructions on salesmanship.

School was over and we two friends packed for our new adventure in Mormon country. Oliver's mother, Grace Jacques, was busy baking a big supply of wheat sticks. She also put up several bottles of grape juice. She included a case of Loma Linda "Ruskets." Later, we found that this extra food kept us from starving! We packed our stuff in Oliver's 1931 Model A car and drove to Los Angeles. This vehicle became our home for three months. We borrowed a pup tent, planning to camp outdoors and sleep in the tent. We also got a gasoline stove so that we could have cooked food.

Deuchene county was high desert country, hot in the day time and cool at night. Saying goodbye to our families, we headed northeast through the great American desert of Nevada and Utah. Our route followed Highway 395, through the Mohave desert to Lone Pine, Bishop and then east to Ely, Nevada. We had to stop for gas where there were only a few houses and one gas station. The old gas pump was a hand-operated model.

While we were resting in the shade, a quaint looking gentleman greeted us. He had very red hair and a long red beard cascading over the bib of his overalls. He carried a black leather bag like those used by physician and took out a pair of roller skates from this bag, put them on and gave an amazing demonstration of his skating skill. After looping the loop on the pavement, he jumped on a picnic table and did a dance, to our delight. You can be sure he got our attention and then asked us for a ride to Wendover, which was on our way to Salt Lake City. We consented and as we continued our journey we were regaled with stories of the Wild West. Our rider claimed to be a physician from New York. He spent his summer traveling the western states, visiting old western hotels looking for and collecting old hotel registers. He was looking for the names of notorious outlaws such as Billy the Kid. Pulling out a register he had just gotten, he showed us the signature of Jesse James. He claimed that back home in New York he had the signature of Wild Bill Hickok. He was quite entertaining.

By the time we got to Wendover, Oliver and I had gotten well acquainted. We drove into Salt Lake City to meet with a group of young men who would be working in Utah. We got more training and picked up books and supplies for the summer. We then drove to Heber City and found a small apartment. This town had hot water springs bubbling out of muddy fumaroles about 20 feet high. Children were swimming in the water!

Oliver and I got ready to begin our canvassing work. On the first morning, I walked around the block a couple of times before getting up the courage to knock on the first door. It was not easy to gain entrance into these Mormon homes. That day Oliver did better than I. We were selling a small medical book for the home and a large print Bible for the elderly. That first day I sold a Bible. When people gave me a hard luck story, I sympathized with them. Neither of us was doing very well. We were glad when our leader, Elder Werner, came to give us more instructions. After a couple of weeks, we ran out of territory; however, we did sell enough to pay the rent, but it was kind of disappointing to realize that selling books was not easy in Mormon country.

To bolster our mood, we bought two oranges. We stood by the car leisurely peeling our oranges, parting each section and enjoying the taste. Oliver finished first and was watching me intently. I spoke up and asked, "Would you like some more?" Oliver burst out laughing. He told me that he was experimenting with mental telepathy. While I was eating my orange, Oliver was concentrating on the thought "Give me a piece." This helped to ease the tension and we had a good time together. In the evenings, as we sat in the tent or around a campfire, Oliver related stories of his great-grandmother's extended family. I enjoyed hearing about the White family and their lifestyle at Rosehaven. Oliver's family had lived with his grandparents, Elder and Mrs. William White, and we talked about the ministry of his great-grandmother, Ellen G. White.

We moved on to new territory that ran east on Highway 40. Some farmers raised alfalfa and other people kept sheep on the range and there were a few dairies. The whole area was watered by ditches fed by creeks coming down from the Wasatch mountains. Those irrigation ditches had clean running water, so Oliver and I camped beside this cooling source of fresh water. The grass grew along the water course and willow trees provided shade. We pitched our tent on the grass, slept in sleeping bags, cooked our food on a gas stove on a box and ironed our pants on the car running board!

One hot day I was taking a short cut across a field when I discovered that I was in the same field as a mean looking Jersey bull. The animal did not take kindly to a stranger on his turf and came thundering down the field, snorting all the way. I headed for the nearest fence. As I slipped through the barbed wire fence, I caught and tore my only good pants. Naomi had given me a little sewing kit that came in handy!

As we worked the desert towns of Deuchene, Roosevelt and White Rocks, we took more book orders. However, we were hearing the farmers complain about lack of rain. Then the grasshoppers came. We continued to take orders, hoping that conditions would get better.

One day while canvassing on the Indian reservation at White Rocks, I had the bright idea of taking Indian artifacts, like moccasins, baskets and clay jars in payment for the books. I told how this health book advised the use of hot and cold water for treatment of medical problems in a manner similar to Indian culture. This lady turned me down, even when I suggested that I would take Indian art objects. She just grunted and shook her head. After a few of these kinds of responses I met with Oliver and found that he had the same results. So we gave up the idea of working with Native Americans who were locally called "Uinta Indians."

While we were in White Rocks, we watched a demonstration of superb horsemanship. A brave, riding his horse at top speed in a field of tall grass, rolled over onto the side of his horse, shot an arrow and then rolled off the horse onto the ground, crawled through the grass, hidden, and then popped up in a different location.

Our final territory was the border town of Vernal. As we entered the little berg, we came to a Sinclair Oil Company station. The company symbol was a large cement replica of a dinosaur about twenty feet tall. We did not know that this town was famous as "Dinosaur National Monument." Later we visited the site where scientists were digging fossil bones of these ancient creatures out from a hillside. Also, many fossils come from the Green River gorge. This river runs along the border between Colorado and Utah.

The Conference office had given us the address of a Mrs. Smith, an Adventist lady who lived in Vernal. She let us make our camp on her spacious lawn under a large shady oak tree. We canvassed the homes in that area and enjoyed fellowship with Mr. and Mrs. Smith who raised minks on their farm. He took us out to see these feisty little creatures. He poked a pencil-sized stick into the cage and they cut it off clean in one bite.

This was the one town we could not get entry into any of the homes. We were getting discouraged. We were not selling very many books and our cash flow was drying up. We were milking cows to get enough milk for our basic needs. Each evening Oliver would go for the milk. I could hear his resonant voice singing, *"Ho Magnum Misterium, Ehtani raubile, Sacramentum."*

One Sabbath Mrs. Smith invited us to a Sabbath dinner of mashed potatoes and gravy, corn on the cob, string beans and apple pie with thick cream and homemade bread. We were the hungriest fellows in the county. In fact, we ate too much for people who had been skimping. That night both of us had stomach aches and lost our whole wonderful meal.

Completing our sales work in Vernal, we then tried to sell at a pitch blend mine a few miles away called "Bonanza Mine." The people were still feeling the results of a drought and the depression. When we went back to deliver the orders we had taken, I had about $400.00 worth of orders, but after four days of no deliveries, we knew that the summer had been a financial failure but a spiritual success. Oliver had orders for more than $500.00 worth of books. We brought back to the Conference a box of new books that we could not deliver.

I owed the Conference about $100.00, so I sold my bike and was almost ready to sell my leather suitcase, but the treasurer would not allow it. He would wait for the C.O.D.s to come in later.

During our stay in Utah, the Conference leaders arranged for the P.U.C. colporteurs to camp near Mt. Nebo south of Salt Lake City. We enjoyed good fellowship and on Sabbath we walked up to Echo Rock. There we organized a quartet and what fun it was to hear the echo of that group. We were able to forget the discouragement of our difficult summer.

Oliver and I headed back across the mountains to Reno, then over the Sierras. The Lord was preparing two young men to take the gospel to Asia and Africa. There would be long treks in the jungle or across the hot sands of the desert. Speaking of Jesus' early life, E. G. White said, "Temptation, poverty, adversity are the very disciplines needed to develop purity and firmness." (DA. p.71) We were ready to begin another school year of training. By Christmas, all the C.O.D.s came in to help pay the debt. Praise the Lord!

Chapter 15

WEDDING BELLS

The fall of Nineteen-Thirty-Nine began with meeting old friends, telling stories of our summer in Utah, and getting acquainted with new students. All of this happened in the hallways or at the dinner table. We were getting oriented to new classes and new teachers.

As a sophomore, I found it was time for me to determine what line of studies I would follow. My choice was ministerial, but what major and minor studies did I need? My counselor helped me decide on a Bible major with a speech and communications minor.

I was putting in more time at the Press, since I was assigned to the press room. I needed to balance my printing skills and interests with more responsibilities in the mailing and binding departments.

Socially, Naomi and I depended on college events to meet each other, so I went to talk to President W. I. Smith to get permission to visit Naomi once a week. I was given a pink slip with the proper signature. We could spend one hour each week visiting in Graf Hall parlor.

So at Christmas time, because Naomi's parents were in Singapore, permission was given for Naomi to go with me to my home in Lynwood, Los Angeles. My Dad came up to get us.

After an enjoyable vacation, we returned to Angwin to begin the new year of 1940. This was to be an important year for us. We talked about our plans for life together in mission service.

"Since both of us were earning our board, room and tuition, wouldn't it be cheaper to pool our resources and get married rather than struggle separately?" At least that was our rationale. We both had good jobs at the school, and Naomi arranged to care for Mrs. Ellis, an invalid, in exchange for the rent of a little cabin down the road. Also, Naomi's sister Betty could stay with us while she attended school. My parents felt that I should wait to complete my education and have assurance of a job. Having known each other for many years and intending to work together in the mission field, Naomi and I set the wedding date for August 18, 1940.

When school was out, I headed for my home in Lynwood, Los Angeles. I went back to work with Ed Rogers' paint crew again. Elmo, my foreman, was a kind man and allowed me to learn the painting trade by giving me specific jobs. Other foremen were pretty harsh in dealing with a young fellow who did not know the trade. One foreman fired me for coming to work in dirty overalls. I went back to the shop and the boss sent me to another job. The painters gave me the dirtiest work to do, like washing filthy kitchen walls with hot lye water, or removing and cleaning inches of thick layers of stinking grease out from under gas stoves in the kitchens. Another job they liked to pass on to the "kid" was cleaning filthy toilets. After working in hot lye all day, my fingers were bleeding. I was glad that my parents had taught me to be patient. Some of the men were not Christians and the stories they told, the language they used was GROSS!

In the middle of the summer of 1940, Adolf Hitler marched his Panzer troops into Belgium. The California economy reacted. I lost my job and set out to pound the sidewalks looking for a job. If I did not find work, we would have to call off the wedding plans. Finally, the right phone call came. It was Ed calling me back to work.

One day I was painting window screens on the roof of a twelve-story apartment building in town. I would take the screens off the windows, carry them up the fire escape to the roof, paint the screens and frames and then carry them back down the fired escaped and set them in the windows again.

The wind was blowing as I carried a screen over the fire wall and onto the fire escape. A sudden gust of wind ripped the screen from my hands, causing it to sail down twelve stories to the sidewalk below. Looking down, my heart skipped a beat as I saw a man walking below. The man did not know a screen, wet with paint, was flying around above his head! Praise the Lord! The screen landed behind the startled man!

That summer I had earned enough for setting up housekeeping and for special needs. As I visited stores in the city that were holding "fire sales," I found a nice navy blue serge suit that had been slightly "smoke damaged." It cost just nineteen dollars and ninety-nine cents. What else? A pair of black Navy surplus shoes, with matching socks and a white shirt. I was all set for the wedding.

Naomi remained in Angwin to make her wedding dress. Her girl friends who were getting married that same summer were sharing expenses by using the same veil. She also saved some dollars while working in Graf Hall kitchen. Her Uncle Fred and Aunt Marion Bowers were taking responsibility for other preparations. Uncle Fred baked and decorated the wedding cake. The wedding was to take place in the "Chapel of the Palms" in Redlands. The reception would be on the Bowers' front lawn. All these plans were coordinated by letter!

Naomi went down to Loma Linda about one week before the big event. Grandpa George Bowers was to give her away. Dad Munson was asked to be the minister. The Bowers had even arranged for a friend to lend us their cabin near Green Valley Lake for our honeymoon.

The chapel was beautifully decorated with two large bouquets of white gladiolas and a backdrop of white lattice with asparagus fern woven through it. A few well placed potted palms completed the decorations. My beautiful bride carried a bouquet of white stephanotis. The wedding was simple, inexpensive but elegant. All the work done by the wedding attendants was unique and beautiful.

About an hour before the wedding, I was in the bathroom shaving and getting ready to dress when suddenly I remembered that I had my Dad's car and my father, the minister, was still at the Redlands park reviewing his sermon! So I rushed out and brought him to the chapel just in time.

Soon we were all ready to go—Albert Munson, myself, and the best man, Oliver Jacques, and groomsmen Harold Hare and Roger Warner.

Elmer Digneo, the organist, played quietly as the wedding guests were ushered into the little chapel. The bride's grandparents were seated in their place to do what the bride's father, Lyman Bowers, had requested. "When Naomi gets married, Dad, you give her away for me." Fred and Marion Bowers, the uncle and aunt of the bride, were proudly representing the bride's parents at the wedding. After that Catherine, the groom's mother, came in on the usher's arm. Then Elmer Digneo played the call for the "Bridal March."

There she stood, in her youthful beauty, with her maid of honor, Betty her sister, and bridesmaids, my sister Iva, and Irma Lee, her college roommate—all ready to lead her down the aisle. On the front row, Grandpa George Bowers sat ready to take his son Lyman's place in giving the bride away.

We exchanged smiles, for our hearts were bursting with pride and joy. For six years we had corresponded, each day looking for that special letter in the mail. Now this was our wedding day. Praise the Lord!

The preacher's sermon was good, dedicating the couple to mission service. The whole program went well. Harriet Skinner, my bride's friend, sang "The Lord's Prayer." Right after the pastoral blessing, we sealed our marriage with a kiss. The minister introduced us as "Mr. and Mrs. George Munson." We were a happy couple among happy and joyful loved ones and friends.

The scene at Uncle Fred's home was full of joy as Naomi and I mingled with our college friends and family. We were seated under a palm tree and the guests were delighted to see a full moon shining on us. Uncle Fred's homemade wedding cake was beautifully decorated and was delicious with ice cream.

As this delightful evening unfolded and guests were leaving, I heard that my cousins and siblings were planning to chase us to the honeymoon cottage. Uncle Fred and I had worked out an escape plan. Fred was to drive us in his car to my father's car, which was locked up in a friend's garage. After the chase car passed the house several times, we jumped

Mr. and Mrs. George Munson

Wedding Party

Future Missionaries

into Fred's car and raced for the hidden vehicle, got into the get-away car and headed for Lake Arrowhead.

I should have scouted the location of the Green Valley Lake cabin earlier. The cabin was painted green and was hard to find in the dark. After driving around for a while, we decided to sleep in the car. Early the next morning we found the cabin tucked away in the woods nearby. We were still in our formal wedding clothes!

It seems that we were being prepared for missionary life, where one has to learn to adapt to all circumstances. We planned to go back to P.U.C., finish our education and head for mission service. I was hoping that it would be Indonesia, my place of birth, but the Lord had other plans for us.

Chapter 16

GRADUATION

Picture a cozy little cabin in the woods, newlyweds beginning a new life, a new bride trying her hand at cooking meals with limited utensils, and adapting the wedding gifts to their new Angwin environment. Naomi and I had invited her sister, Betty Bowers, to stay with us. It was her first year of college. Since Naomi was working for our housing, we were able to earn enough cash for groceries.

I was working around the yard, cutting and watering the plants and trees to make the place look better. I even tried a spring garden to grow a few salad greens.

Another occupant of our little cabin was Bibi, the Ellis's black water Spaniel. He was a source of laughter and fun. We lived about a mile from the college, so the whole family did a lot of walking. On Sabbath afternoon we enjoyed strolling down Howell Mountain road as Bibi challenged us to throw rocks into the creek so he could retrieve them. Sometimes he dove in after rocks that were too heavy and he had to struggle up the bank to deposit the load at our feet. On the road one rock was so heavy it lifted his hind legs when he tried to move it!

All of us were busy with our studies every evening. Sometimes Bibi would stand up in front of us with his front paws up, begging for food or whatever he wanted.

The rains came early that winter and we walked to school in wet shoes for twenty days! We took cardboard from Shredded Wheat boxes and cut them to make innersoles to fit our shoes.

But with spring came the inspiration to begin a back yard garden on the hill behind the cabin. It was fun to work in the warm sun and dig in the soil and see the tiny vegetable plants grow, with dreams of some day having our own garden to till. It was a new year and very important for us. Naomi worked at the college store soda fountain, fixing drinks and making sandwiches. My work at the Press had increased. I was operating the big Miehle flatbed press running the Pacific Union Recorder. We were having a good year and were asked to take heavier responsibilities while older and younger men were fighting in the Pacific War.

On June 1, 1941, in Jesselton, Borneo, Lyman and Ella Mae Bowers were celebrating their 25th wedding anniversary by inviting friends Dr. Liem and his wife, to their home for dinner. In a letter they said they "used the new silverware." Then on June 13 they celebrated Lyman's 48th birthday. Three days later, Ella Mae had a chill. The next morning she had a fever so did not get up, but later felt better. They were wondering if it was "dengue" fever. On the 18th Lyman took her temperature and found it was 104.2. By Sabbath morning the fever had gone down some. She felt better. They spent a quiet day reading the "Review." That evening, about 8:00 p.m. the fever increased and she lapsed into a coma, which continued. Lyman called two doctors but it was too late. She opened her eyes towards heaven, and little by little her breathing ceased. Lyman says, "My comrade sleeps." They loved each other dearly. Their local friends in the community were a great help to the grieving husband. From Father Lyman's notes he quotes that Elder Diris Siagian, a Batak missionary, led in the funeral service and that he was comforted by the national workers and European friends with whom he had been holding Bible studies.

He sent five telegrams, one of which his daughter Betty received. This was followed with letters to Naomi, Betty and myself. We were impressed with the fact that Lyman continued faithfully to preach in the village churches and carry on his work as Mission president for another two months He left North Borneo July 30 after visiting the little grave on the hillside cemetery where his dearest friend and lover awaits the resurrection morning.

Here is Lyman Bowers's poem of comfort at his wife's death:

THE SUNSET HOUR

Long since had fled the morning mist
And gone the torrid heat of noon;
The wind is still, and past the shower,
Ah! 'Tis the glorious sunset hour!
    The day perchance a little long,
    And burden heavy you have borne;
    Yet straight and wise a path you chose,
    Which guards the hours of sweet repose.
Our life like days doth ever change,
Some hours are dark and some are light,
God knows us each,—He sends what's best—
And lo, at eve, He gives sweet rest.
    Like ships, that cross the ocean wide,
    "Mid storm and gale and starless night,
    At last reach port—from fear release,
    Where all is calm, where all is peace
There's fragrance in life of years,
Well spent in kind and noble deeds;
A buoyant life—strength from above,
With friends, companionship and love.
    Confiding as the song of birds,
    Calm as the ripple of the waves,
    Unending as the stars endure,
    E'en so has been His promise sure.
To learn the lesson of the years,
To trust and wait, nor doubt His love,
To let Him all your burden bear,
Is but to come to Him in prayer.
    For life thus filled with blessings rich,
    Which outshine honor, wealth, or fame;
    Unto Thy throne my eyes I raise,
    To give Thee all my heartfelt praise.
Thoughts of home are in the breast—
A home to welcome all who come;
Where heart is knit in love to heart;
That Home from which we ne'er shall part.

"At even time it shall be light",
Transcending e'en the sunsets' glow!
Dispelling doubt, sin, and sorrow,
Ah! A glimpse of God's tomorrow!

Lyman Bowers was a faithful personal worker, keeping a prayer list of interested friends who bought the books "The Great Controversy," "Patriarchs and Prophets," and "The Desire of Ages." He prepared them spiritually even including his spiritual son, Won Sung. At the funeral he prayed that these people would meet his beloved Ella Mae in heaven.

It was 1941. Naomi would graduate with an Elementary Education Certificate. I went to the Press manager, requesting a raise in wages from 22 cents per hour to 25 cents. I was turned down.

The day for Naomi's graduation came. Uncle Paul and Aunt Francis Munson came up from Napa to attend the ceremony. I had been running the big press all night and looked like a zombie. Uncle leaned over and asked me how much I was getting per hour to work at the Press. I responded, "Twenty-two cents." Uncle Paul said, "Don't be foolish. Come and work for me and I'll give you ninety cents per hour for painting houses with me." I accepted the challenge. In one week I was painting houses in Napa.

Our family budget was really improved by this move. After working all summer and earning a decent wage, we made an important decision. Since we needed inexpensive housing and needed to build up credit at the school, I decided to stay out of school one semester, buy a small plot of land and build a little cabin. We moved into a small apartment at Merle Vance's apartment complex. He had built several small apartments in his home for students.

That year we decided to buy a small quarter acre of land from Merle. That fall as I worked in Napa I would get my pay on Friday, spend part of it on building supplies and haul it to Angwin on the roof of my 1930 Chevy. I stockpiled the boards on our lot and on Sundays prepared to build our cabin. There was a building supply place at Napa Nee. Knotty pine boards, shiplap and 2x4s all cost just three cents per foot. Also secondhand plumbing and building supplies were cheap.

Naomi and I experienced the excitement of drawing plans for our little cottage, our first home! On Sunday we had a new experience digging footings and pouring the foundation. By the first of December the cement was cured enough to complete the floor joists and sub floor.

Sunday morning, December 7, we were up early, eager to set up the first framed wall of our 20' x 20' cabin. We measured and cut the boards and soon were nailing the studs together. Naomi helped me raise the wall and as I raised my hammer to nail in a brace when suddenly someone came running up to the site, crying bitterly. It was my sister Iva. Between her sobs we learned that the Japanese had bombed Pearl Harbour! My Mother and Father had gone to Hawaii earlier that year and we were concerned about our parents' safety. As Civilian Chaplain for servicemen and women, Dad was responsible for their spiritual needs. He jumped into his sedan and drove to the entrance gate of Hickam Air Force Base. The car was suddenly an ambulance transporting wounded sailors and airmen to the Tripler Hospital above the hill. Dad spent the evening unsuccessfully cleaning caked blood from the mohair upholstery. For nine more years, Albert and Katie Munson faithfully served the men and women of the armed forces.

The whole nation rallied to President Roosevelt's "Day of Infamy" call to respond to the aggression of Japan. Soon our college friends were called one by one to serve. I received my call from the Draft Board but was given exemption as a ministerial student and for physical reasons. My Japanese classmates and friends were being hauled off into the hot western deserts to suffer in concentration camps. I felt so sorry for them. Overnight, gasoline and other critical supplies needed in the war effort were rationed. Women were taking the place of men in factories and farms.

Work on our cabin was progressing, but soon it was hard to buy building supplies, for everything was going to the war effort. I was purchasing secondhand plumbing supplies, sink and toilet and hand-blown glass windows from a century-old house. I had planned ahead and purchased critical supplies like electric wire and fixtures.

While working for Uncle Paul, I ate lunch with the builders and asked them many questions. I learned how to brace walls, why the fire blocks in the walls, what size of pipes to use for sewer lines and bathrooms and other building code issues. I bought a Sears "How To" book on wiring the house. The first circuit I wired blew the fuse! Finally I got it right and the house did not burn down!

We were getting anxious about moving into our home sometime in 1942. We lugged our stuff up from Merle's apartment house. There wasn't much—an old rusty bed spring, a lumpy mattress, and a couple of rickety chairs.

We had lined all rooms, including the ceilings, with knotty pine and sealed it with shellac. The outside of the cabin was finished with shiplap a foot wide which looked nice with a couple of coats of paint. The remaining boards were used for cabinets and window framing. Not knowing how to set the toilet and build a septic tank, I did not have these jobs done before we moved in.

Naomi was pregnant with our first baby. We tried to make things as comfortable as possible. We found a fine looking wood space heater to install in the living room. This made things cozy and warm during that first winter. An old dresser was in the bedroom and a small table and chairs in the kitchen served to make us comfortable.

Not long after we moved in, we got a great Christmas present from the Lord. Our first baby, Ruth Eloise, was born on December 28, 1942. Being our first birth experience, we got to the St. Helena Hospital early. We did not know it then, but the baby was not sure she wanted to greet the world out there. Her mother struggled in labor for 22 hours! Joyfully we brought her home to Bob and Millie Reiger's apartment. As Naomi lay on the divan with the baby in her arms, I picked up our baby and held her. What an experience!

In the summer of 1943, those living on Diogenes Drive got an awful scare. Since we had lived at Vance's apartments we were friends with Doc and Frankie Layland. He was taking pre-med and they had their baby a few weeks earlier. One warm summer evening we were playing croquet on our front lawn and the baby girls were in their bassinets in our living room. Suddenly someone was shouting, "Fire! Fire!" We dropped our mallets and ran towards the apartment house. Flames were pouring out of the windows of the house and had ignited the tar paper lining. Doc and I ran down the stairs and tried to move appliances out of the kitchen, but the doors were too small. As Frankie ran to help her husband to rescue things in their apartment, she called out to Naomi, "Take care of my baby." Naomi called back that she was putting both babies in the car to drive to a safe place. She watched the fire from across the valley. Vance called for everybody to leave the burning building (for the thick black smoke was toxic). They gathered outside waiting for the fire department to arrive. The 250-gallon propane tank was shooting a forty-foot flame into the sky with a frightening roar, threatening to explode any minute.

When I saw the light wind whipping the fire into the dry grass towards our house, I ran, grabbed a hose, climbed up the ladder and stuffed wet rags through the open attic door. I closed the door and climbed onto the roof to hose things down in case the fire spread. As I was wetting down the roof the fire truck arrived. The fireman asked if they should try to save our house, but I told him to get the big house first.

It was a sad group of people who stood in the light of the dying embers of that fire. Three families were homeless! The question was, "Where shall we sleep tonight?" The Perrin's parents took them in; the Laylands went to their relatives, and the Vance family stayed with Naomi and me.

Merle and I turned the attic of Vance's barn into an apartment for temporary housing. Everyone found a comfortable spot.

In the fall of '43, Harold Clark, editor of the "Campus Chronicle," cornered me and prevailed on me to become the campaign manager of the "Campus Chronicle" subscription campaign. The student body usually had a hilarious time during this effort. Sides were chosen, the Blue and the Gray. With clever skits, promotion banners and the general excitement of this campaign, the student body gained a lot of sub-scriptions for the school paper that year.

The year of Forty-Four began with final preparations for me to finish my studies and graduate. Because of the war ef-fort, critical gasoline rations were in short supply for my 56-mile round trip drive to work. So one day I stopped in St. Hel-ena at Fred Knipschild's machine shop to ask for a job. Fred had a few College boys working for him and liked their work. He asked me how much I was earning and hired me at the same rate to paint the shop and work on the welding jobs.

When gasoline was getting harder to get I began mixing kerosene in the gas tank. This made the engine very sluggish and finally ruined the valves on our 1934 Chevy sedan. A few months before graduation the fuel problem became critical, so I quit Knipschild's and found painting jobs on the hill. Merle Vance hired me for a few months to build him a new house. Merle was still working at Mare Island shipyard and was able to stockpile a good supply of 2 x 12 boards he had purchased from the yard. First, we helped him convert his 1936 Ford coupe into a pickup so that he could haul 2x12s from Mare Island. Then we staked out the foundation for a three-bedroom cottage. We used abundant local field stones for the foundation. Merle worked with me on Sundays. We built a 30" saw mill to process the 2 x 12s. In a few weeks we had the house framed in and the roof beams finished. Upon completion the Vances moved into their three-bedroom home with one bath and a large attic storage space. I also helped drill the well for the home which provided us with a much-needed water right.

To keep the family in food, I continued with small paint jobs. At one point we were several weeks without work. The cupboard was getting bare and we had only tithe money with some change. Baby Eloise needed milk. Should we use the tithe or wait on the Lord? We paid the tithe that Sabbath. On Sunday, I got a phone call asking me to paint a house. The Lord says, "Bring the whole tithe into the storehouse, that there may be food in my house. Test me in this, says the Lord Almighty." Micah 3:10.

Lloyd Irving was born on May 3, 1944, just one month before my graduation, so I got a "P.A." as well as a B.A. diploma at that ceremony. We praised the Lord for the wonderful little family.

Along with the diploma we got four letters from Conference presidents offering us positions in their Conferences. I had hoped to return to Indonesia where three members of the family had served, but the political situation was not stable.

So since it was on the way to Asia, we accepted Elder George Taylor's invitation to work as an intern in Hawaii. I would pastor Wahiawa church on Central Oahu. Since we were leaving for Hawaii, we decided to sell our little cabin at cost. However, we told the buyer that if he planned to sell at some future time we wanted to buy it back. He got a bargain.

For twelve years I had been suffering with a congenital double hernia. Sometimes I had to stop heavy work to push the intrusion in. When I reported this to the Mission leaders, they agreed for me to have surgery upon arrival in the islands. They also had a car for me to buy.

Since the war was not over, travelers had to get special papers to go by ship to Hawaii. While waiting for these arrangements, we packed our few belongings, including our bed, my desk and file cabinet which I had built in college cabinet class, a crib for the baby and a few family items. Men could travel to the islands but women and children were not allowed yet.

It was a slow trip by convoy, chugging along at 10 knots with a destroyer escort that zig-zagged all the way. We were told that Japanese submarines were lurking.

The accommodations were crowded, but in the evening, with no lights, the passengers sat on deck, listening to the Hawaiians "talk story" and strum their ukuleles as they sang native island ballads. No one could smoke, for the light of a cigarette could be seen a mile away.

The ship rounded Diamond Head and entered the Aloha Harbor. It was good to see the lovely islands with lines of coconut trees and to smell the fragrant aroma of tropical flowers. Our mission internship was beginning.

Chapter 17

AFTER PEARL HARBOUR

Upon arriving in Hawaii, I was impressed with the friendly welcome we received. Since I had arrived by a convoy of Liberty ships three months before Naomi and the children, I stayed with Mom and Dad in their home at Kaimuki. Dad was busy with his work as Civilian Chaplain. Since the war in the Pacific was winding down, he helped to entertain many servicemen and women.

Every Sabbath my Mom and several ladies of the Keeaumoku Central SDA church prepared a delicious Sabbath dinner for about forty or more Adventist service personnel. Hundreds of World War II veterans still remember Mother Munson's delicious homemade gluten steaks with brown gravy, mashed potatoes, green peas, and salad, complete with apple pie and ice cream! These men and women were the guests of the Central Church in Honolulu where Elder Walde was pastor.

One day, Dad asked me if I would like to go seashell hunting with him and some G.I.s. Of course I eagerly joined them but I forgot that the California sun and the Hawaiian tropical ultraviolet rays were very different! After diving for shells off Waikiki, I lay down on the sand in the shadow of a coconut tree and woke up two hours later with a super sunburn—so bad I was in bed for a week!

The Mission had purchased a car for me but the battery was dead, the tires were flat, and the vehicle needed lots of work. When the car was in running order, I drove out to visit the little Wahiawa church I was to pastor. I made arrangements to stay with the treasurer's family, Brother John Kim and his wife Saddie.

In preparation for Naomi's and the kids' arrival, I searched for temporary housing. It was not easy since the town was close to Schofield Army Base, and many service families were occupying any available houses. Finally I found a little two-room cabin with a bath and kitchenette that belonged to a businessman and member of the church. When I stepped into the front room, large roaches scurried all over the room. Then as I walked around, fleas crawled over my legs and shoes. We finally controlled the critters with chemicals! The place had a double garage and an orchard of forty apple banana trees. We ate lots of bananas while living there.

While waiting for my family to arrive and before beginning pastoral work, the Mission wanted me to get my double hernia surgery. So I saw the doctor and entered Queens hospital for the operation. A spinal was given to prepare me for surgery. As he was operating, the doctor told me it would be better to have my appendix removed, especially if I was going to be in Borneo as a missionary. As I watched them fumbling with those pink organs, I said, "I feel like throwing up." Right away the nurse gave me oxygen, pulled up the sheet, and administered some ether so I would not be affected by the operation. I woke up lying in bed in a large ward. A nun came to my bedside and told me not to get out of bed for one week or I'd get a bad headache. There was a Puerto Rican in the bed next to me, and he kept making everyone laugh, painfully. Then he jumped out of bed, which caused him to suffer headaches, so he was groaning all the time. He got over the problem, but his constant joking put stress on our stitches!

After recuperating from surgery, I went to Wahiawa, but before I settled into pastoral work a strange thing happened. Boils broke out under my armpit. In a short time there were thirteen painful boils that needed medical attention!

At summer's end the rest of the family came by convoy from San Francisco. I was glad to see Naomi and the two children, Eloise and Lloyd, standing on the deck of that Navy transport. Before going out to Wahiawa, we spent time with Mother and Dad in Kaimuki. They showed the family around the island, visiting the Pali with its steady wind, the famous Punch Bowl and military cemetery, and the golden sands of Kailua Beach.

After spending the weekend in Honolulu, we returned to our cabin and again large cockroaches scattered everywhere. As we walked around, fleas jumped on our legs. The pests were finally controlled. We stayed there while the Mission contractor built a new parsonage next to the church.

One evening as I was painting something in the garage, I heard the roar of a B-25 making an approach to Wheeler Field. I stepped out just in time to see this bomber hitting the tops of tall eucalyptus trees. Sparks were flying and the pilot was losing altitude fast. The plane dove into the ground just a few hundred yards beyond John Kim's home. John ran out with his ax but could not rescue the airmen—the burning gasoline was too hot and the men perished!

The first Sabbath in Wahiawa we met a multi-ethnic group of about 125 church members. Thirty-five were of Korean ancestry. Naomi was at home with them since she was born and raised in their ancestral home. There were Chinese, Filipino and Japanese families and of course families of Hawaiian descent. Then there was a Caucasian family, Elder John Heaton and his wife and daughters who had served in Hawaii as literature evangelists. He and his wife had given Bible studies to hundreds of people in the islands and had raised up the Wahiawa congregation. So we had a unique opportunity with this wonderful group who gave the young pastor and family such a warm welcome.

The first elder of the church was Brother Ben Leialoha. He had been sitting at the feet of Elder Heaton. He knew the "Church Manual" and was well trained in Bible doctrines. He had given Bible studies to people who were now members. Ben ran a "tight ship." This was a great help to a young intern. His wife, Elanore, cheerfully took on jobs in the church and served well. Their children were Ben Junior, Rose, Lemuel and young Waletta.

Mrs. Heaton was a real "Mother of Israel." She worked hard to keep the church spic-and-span. She would get on a ladder and make sure that all the glass windows and doors were polished. She would even clean up after the myna birds when they dirtied the sidewalks. She worked with Brother Garcia, the custodian, and encouraged him to mop all the floors and wax them with red wax. We came to a very clean church each Sabbath. What an example to our congregation. One Friday, I asked Brother Garcia why he worked so hard in cleaning the church. He replied, "For da God!"

When we began work in Wahiawa, I felt that I should connect with the community so that our congregation could supply the felt needs of the people around them. We are not here just to give a warning but to invite the people to the joys of knowing Jesus and enjoying the Lord's blessings. So I joined the Junior Chamber of Commerce. I was their chaplain and when they ate lunch together each Tuesday, they asked me to offer the blessing.

The members of the J.C.s learned that we had a boys' club and they made donations of tools and funds for the club. Also they donated a club house, an Army surplus cabin for the youth. I helped the boys build a kayak and this made their youth picnics more enjoyable.

Soon the J.C.s had a request for me: "Please establish a pre-school so that our children can have early education." The request was brought to the church board, and they decided to build two classrooms, expand the playground and bring in another teacher. Naomi agreed to organize the program with Elanore Leialoha as assistant. The men of the church planned to help build the classrooms and restrooms for the children. It was 1945, and the islands did not have a supply of lumber to sell. Everybody was using the surplus lumber from the armed forces. This was used dunnage and airplane boxes. We bought a pile of this material for $150.00. It took a whole month just to pull the 20d nails out of the stuff. Finally, we were ready to call the men of the church to work on Sundays and build the school rooms. They used Cainex for wallboard inside, and special waterproof Cainex for the exterior walls. Our men did the electrical work, plumbing, and painting. The floors were cement and the men did a fine job in finishing the work.

The surplus boards were used to build the restrooms for the boys and girls All of the work passed the approval of the building inspector. We put up chalk boards and display bulletins as well as chairs and little beds for the tiny tots' use at rest time.

We were proud of the men and women who did the work on the school. They hauled in several truckloads of crushed coral and covered the parking lot and playground. They also made playground equipment. Now all was ready for twenty students. However, more than twenty applied but all were gladly accepted!

Naomi and her assistant, Elanore Leialoha, prepared the programs well. The men at the J.C. club were delighted and sent the children to school. In fact Miss Mary Elquist, who was our grade school teacher, had so many students she arranged for her mother to come and teach in a second classroom.

While Naomi conducted the pre-school, it was my duty to care for our young children in the morning. This meant going for walks, supervising their play and yes, changing diapers! Sometimes they would get my attention with howls like a train whistle!

The church family was growing, and the church board members were making plans to hold public evangelistic meetings. Several of the members had been trained by Elder Heaton to give Bible studies to people who accepted Jesus as their Saviour. They wanted to be involved in church planting. I talked to my fellow intern, George Kiyabu, about the best place to begin such a program. Brother Kiyabu said he had a group of youth in Aiea who were already studying the Voice of Prophecy lessons together. We decided to ask the Mission for the evangelistic tent and for funds to begin. Elden Chalmers and Walter Barber wanted to begin meetings on the island of Kauai. They needed the tent, too.

Wahiawa started the ball rolling by inspiring their members to begin the campaign in the town of Aiea. The Mission committee voted to help and when they arranged with Dole Canning Company for the lease of their property, the members of the Mission committee came out on a Sunday and helped pitch the old tent.

In Aiea, the youth group studying the Bible had built a little shelter with pineapple crates. They were diligently study-

Wahiawa Church
Paster—Albert Munson; Intern—George Munson

George Kiyabu, manager; George Munson, speaker;
Pastor Albert Munson, advisor; brother Alapai,
singing evangelist

Our team on the platform, ready for action

ing with Brother Kiyabu and an American soldier named Gordon Collier. We visited the group and were encouraged by the sight of these young people led by Kenneth Kakazu. The Holy Spirit was leading them into a special experience.

Once the tent was pitched, the youth came out to help rake wood chips for the tent floor and paint the panels the Wahiawa group had constructed. They used plywood-like Cainex four-by-eight foot panels to build the platform and front façade of the tabernacle. They decorated the white platform panels with painted Cainex cutout letters, "PREPARE TO MEET THY GOD."

A load of white coral was spread out for the entrance walkway, and we were ready for the meetings.

Ben Leialoha led the Wahiawa members in visiting, ushering and other details. George Kiyabu was general manager and in charge of visiting and follow-up Bible studies. My Father gave advice and illustrated the sermons I preached.

While I was preaching the lesson on Daniel 2, Dad drew the image of Nebuchadnezzar's dream. It was a very good attention-holding element with the audience.

There was opposition to the meetings. Someone smeared human feces on the pulpit then wrote graffiti on the walls of the tent. Because of this vandalism, the Kakazu boys decided they should sleep near the platform. One night someone came in and started a fire in the boys' clothing and wood chips. The boys woke up and put out the fire. Then, one night while I was preaching, a drunk sailor walked in and started shouting and mimicking the words of the preacher. Ben Leialoha stepped up and gave the drunk the "bouncer's" lock step right out of the tent!

Satan's last trick was sending a poor mother into the tent crying uncontrollably. It seems she had been playing with the Hawaiian Kahuna (witchcraft). Her home was troubled with weird rappings, and her baby was crying uncontrollably, like someone was choking it with unseen hands. Her husband was terrified and ran away. So she came for help. Brother Kiyabu worked with this family and the group of believers spent all night praying for the child. Praise the Lord! He brought peace to the home.

That first evangelistic campaign resulted in the baptism of the Kakazu family. Altogether twenty-five young people took their stand to follow Jesus. The little congregation was led by George Kiyabu. The tent was dismantled and sent to Kauai for the meetings there. Then they bought Army surplus buildings and raised their first church on rented property. Today a congregation of about four hundred members worships in a fine church just across the highway from the old property. My son Lloyd with Jeanne his wife pastored the church sixty years later.

When the Mission tent came back to Oahu, the Wahiawa members helped us with another evangelistic series in the town of Haleiwa. There was already an Adventist family holding meetings in their home near this area. They rented a piece of land right next to the local Congregational church, across from Matsumoto's "shave ice." The meetings were attended by several local youth.

In local Hawaiian-style hospitality, we sat on grass mats on the ground under a coconut tree. The sea breeze was gently stroking our cheeks and the scent of flower leis was intoxicating. The hostess brought bowls of three finger poi, a generous serving of fresh fish just caught in the lagoon nearby, and lots of local fruit like apple bananas, mangos, and custard apples. We did well on consuming the poi and fruit but lost courage on downing fresh fish, which brought peals of friendly laughter!

Heavy rain nearly spoiled the Haleiwa meetings. We tried to waterproof the old tent with paraffin, but it did not work. The good people of Haleiwa were very patient. The meetings ended with a baptism of ten from local families and their friends.

Another group of fine young people came to Wahiawa after the members had given them Bible studies. They were the children of pineapple workers of Camp Robinson. To visit them for Bible studies, I had to drive through a restricted Army ammunition storage area. One night the M.P. stopped me and his Doberman guard dog gave me a scare when it charged the window. Continuing on to the plantation, I had a good Bible study with the teenagers. During the study, a heavy tropical rain drenched the pineapple fields. My little Studebaker Champion could not get up the hill on the slick, red clay road. I had to get out and push the car out of several mud holes. I was sopping wet—rolled up pants covered with mud—and shirtless when I finally stumbled into the kitchen at home.

Our very active Pathfinder club met in a donated cabin. For crafts, the boys were taught how to make koa wood bowls and other items to give to their families. They constructed a nine-foot-kayak and took it to the north shore to learn water safety and other camping skills as they enjoyed picnics on the beach.

One day I borrowed a small truck to pick up some donated koa wood and plywood for the boys' shop. As I drove out of town, I heard church bells ringing, then sirens, and finally car horns honking. People were pouring out of the shops into the streets, shouting, "THE WAR'S OVER!" We stopped the truck in the middle of the road—for it was full of people shouting, "Victory! Victory! We have won!"

Near the end of the war the armed forces were gathering tanks and other heavy materials and equipment in preparation for shipment back to the mainland. The roads from the military bases to the ships and planes were used so heavily by tanks and half-tracks they were full of potholes and were rapidly breaking down. We had used our car to go to town so much that it was badly in need of repairs. When the extensive mechanical repairs were completed, I suggested they paint it as well. When I got the bill it was a staggering $750.00, more than the original price of the car. What to do? With embarrassment I went to the Mission treasurer, Joe Emmerson. He was kind. He looked at the blue paint job and tried out the car and said, "I'll buy it from you." He paid the bill and I began looking for cheaper transportation. One of our church members had an old rusty Model A, which he sold to me for $150.00. So we ran around in a topless coupe.

In the spring of 1946, I received a phone call from Hickam Air Force Base. It was Elder R. S. Watts, Senior, an old friend of Naomi's family from their mission days in Korea. He told me he would be in Honolulu for only a short time and had a burden on his mind. World War II had ended and he was asked by the General Conference to be president of the Korean Union. He was flying the next day to Manila to join the leaders of the Far Eastern Division in a planning session at Baguio. He asked me if we would accept a call as missionaries to Korea. Since I had training and experience in the publishing field, he wanted me to be manager of the Korean Signs of the Times Publishing House. The Division would send us to California for me to take special training at the Pacific Press in Mountain View. When the military in Korea would allow civilians to enter, I would go to build up the press in Seoul. Watts gave us twelve hours to decide! Naomi and I spent a long night in prayer, discussion and heart searching.

The next morning when Ralph Watts called, we said, "Yes," we would go to Korea as missionaries. We were asked to proceed to Mountain View to get a year of special upgrading and training at the Pacific press. Then as the military government allowed it, I would go on to Seoul, ahead of the family, to begin work at rebuilding the publishing house located at the Mission headquarters.

Naomi's father, Lyman Bowers, lived in Mountain View with his wife Delphine and worked at the Press. Since Naomi was going to be in the area for a while, Lyman converted his shop into a little apartment for the family. I worked at the Press starting in the press room with Lyman. I studied the different types of presses and folding machines and worked with Stanley Hall in the engraving department, then moved to the type composition department. I had the opportunity to try the different machines and processes in the bindery. Learning the methods of marbling the edges of large books was fun. Then I moved on to the finance office to learn accounting procedures.

The art department was where magazines and books were done in the layout room. Mr. Maramontes was in charge and I spent some time in this department, since it was my special interest. This experience was useful in the Seoul plant when it came time to lay out the new Korean "Signs" where I made a drawing of a young Korean man saluting his new national flag.

The Pacific Press presented to the Korean Press some equipment and supplies to help in the functions of the Korean plant. Arrangements were made by the Ace Packing and Shipping Company in San Francisco for the equipment to be shipped by freight to Korea.

One day I had a load of smaller equipment and supplies to be packed and shipped, so I loaded them in my old 1928 Dodge. I was driving about 45 miles per hour towards San Francisco when suddenly in my rearview mirror I saw the lights of a car approaching at a high speed and then C–R–A–S–H! The driver hit me with a powerful blow! My little old sedan leaped forward as I struggled to control it.

When the car finally stopped, I got out to assess the damage and saw a late model Buick with the radiator and lamps trashed. The radiator was losing steam and water. The driver was unhurt but his passenger had hit the windshield with his head so his forehead was bleeding. The driver, who had liquor on his breath, said he did not see the Dodge and that my car did not have its lights on.

In a few minutes the CHP arrived to help settle the problem. He observed that the Dodge did have tail lights and that there were plenty of red reflectors on the rear of the car. The officer wrote down his report and suggested that the man with the injured head go to the local clinic to be treated. He asked if my car was operable, which it was, and I followed the officer to the nearby clinic. The officer tested the driver of the Buick and gave a citation for DUI.

The spare tire on the back of my Dodge was flat and imprinted on the trunk of the car. The rear window was smashed in tiny shards. Inside the car, a five-gallon can of shellac had burst open and splashed all over the interior.

It was already late when I left the clinic, so I decided to get a hotel room in San Francisco. I found that I was low in cash so rented a dollar room for the night. The fleas and bedbugs stole my night of sleep! I did not know it then, but I had suffered a whiplash. The next morning at home I could not get out of bed! Naomi helped me get up and took me to the St. Helena Hospital for hydrotherapy treatment and medication.

After completion of my training at the Press, I was asked to join another mission appointee, Walter Knittle, to study the Korean language at UC/Berkeley. Our young Korean teacher lived in Mountain View, so we rode together to the University. Our teacher, John Lee, was an opera singer so we were well entertained during our trips from Mt. View to Berkeley and home.

In the spring of 1947, we returned to our little cottage in Angwin to pack the family freight for shipment to Korea and also to get repairs done on our house and get the family settled. Since we did not know when the family would join me, I did my best to make things easy for Naomi by preparing the garden and planting vegetables.

Word came that Brother Robert Mills, the new Korean Union Treasurer, from Chattanooga would be sailing with me from San Francisco on the Navy hospital ship, "S.S. Hope." When Bob and I got our cabins, we found ourselves assigned to the psychiatric ward at the stern of the ship!

The third week of June, Bob and I joined the Munson and Bowers families on board the ship for a traditional farewell to departing missionaries. Everyone was impressed with this famous vessel and had a good laugh about the assignment of our cabin—at least it wasn't the brig.

As they parted, some members of the family said they would be waving goodbye from the Golden Gate Bridge. Of course my Mom cried, but she joined Dad in praising the Lord that a third generation of Munsons was going to Asia. They promised to pray for me every day. (I knew how that would be, because one day, when I walked into their home in Sunnyside, I found them having family worship, like they had done all of their lives. They were singing a hymn in the Malay language and as I joined them, Dad prayed in the Indonesian language.)

Chapter 18

WAR IN KOREA

Early Sunday morning, June 25, 1950, the men were awakened by the howling of sirens. They looked at their watches, groaned, and promptly went back to sleep. Army trucks were rolling down the highway. Finally someone woke up and asked, "What's going on?" In their Korean hotel room they slowly came to consciousness. The men from Seoul mumbled to each other. They were: Ernst Bahr, Union president; Kim Sang Chill, secretary; Bob Mills, treasurer; Pak Chang Uk, associate treasurer; James Lee, College president; and myself, Press manager. One by one they got up and went out to the well in the courtyard to shave in cold water. OUCH!

We all dressed and sat down to wait for breakfast, but nothing happened. Mr. Pak clapped sharply and a timid manager poked his head in the door and with a low bow told the group, "Last night the army confiscated all the rice in town. We have no breakfast." That was our first clue that it would be a day of serious crisis! After some negotiating, the ladies of the church kindly provided some of the rice cakes from the dedication dinner of the day before.

The Korean Union leaders from Seoul had come on Thursday to Kangnung to dedicate the first church to be built in Korea after World War II.

We men knew that there was a U.S. Army advisory group stationed nearby. We finished our meager breakfast quickly and hurried over to meet with Sergeant Bonapart, a burly Texan. He thrust out his big hand and drawled: "Wheah yeawl been?" We replied, "What's going on?" "Well," he said, "it turns out the Communist Army of North Korea just last night crossed the 38th Parallel and is attacking South Korea along the front line. Just this morning they successfully landed on the beach near Kangnung. You boys better high-tail it outa heah now. On your way out look out for special troops hiding along the way." Immediately we returned to the hotel, packed our bags and called for a meeting at the church. There were tears as we worshiped the Lord and bade goodbye to the members and local pastors attending the celebration.

Our troubles had just begun—our car was out of gas, a couple of tires were flat, and the battery was dead! James Lee scurried to get gasoline, others started to repair tires, and somebody got emergency tools to use on the road since the monsoon rains had already started. We pushed the car to get the battery built up, then all six squeezed into the car and waved farewell to the believers. Each one would have a unique war experience to tell later.

We passed a Korean Army truck loaded with young civilian men singing war songs. Each one carried sharpened bamboos to face an enemy with machine guns. All morning we heard machine gun fire and the crunch of mortar shells. When we saw these brave youth, we did not know then that hundreds of thousands would bleed on the battle fields of Korea. One of the group wanted to stop and take a picture, but I replied, "Don't you think it is more important to get to our families in Seoul as soon as we can?"

It was pouring down rain when we started up the steep famous Tae Kwalyoung Pass. The Korean Army trucks had dug deep ditches in the red clay road. Bob Mills was struggling to keep the car wheels out of the ruts and the car from rolling down into the steep canyon. All of the men agreed that the angels of heaven were pushing the car rapidly up the hill! We did not slide off once or get stuck in the mud! Praise the Lord!

Darkness fell as we rounded the last switchback of that treacherous mountain road. Again the Lord had gone before us, for there had been a landslide across the road, but the Korean Army had gone ahead and cleared the way. All six of us silently prayed that we would be able to pass the Army checkpoint at the provincial town of Heungsung. We were stopped and told that for our own safety we could not go on as a tank battle was taking place in the next valley. We told the officer we were expected in Seoul and could take the southern route to avoid the battle. Finally, receiving permission, we climbed back into the car, thanking the Lord for another opening. The

roads were rough and full of large rocks, the result of churn-
ing tanks. The Lord preserved the tires. Flashes of cannon
fire lit up the hills. We learned later that the South Korean
Sherman tanks could not match the Russian tanks as they
dueled just down the road to Chunchon.

We arrived in the outskirts of Seoul, after cutting our return trip by two hours. Due to blackout conditions, the streets
were unfamiliar, though the going was slow. We had to drive
very carefully as we met the Korean cavalry moving into
positions outside of the city. The horses had machine guns
strapped to their backs and were camouflaged with brush.
As we slowly moved into Huigyung Dong, a Buick came up
to the men and Dr. Ralph Pearson called out, "It's about time
you men got here. The U.S. Embassy has ordered all wom-
en and children to be ready to evacuate by two-thirty a.m."
This spurred us on to the gates of the Union compound. They
sounded the usual "Beep-beep." The wives heard the familiar
call and came rushing out of their homes.

I found that Naomi had packed three suitcases, one for
Eloise and Lloyd, one for baby Bonnie, our one-year-old who
needed diapers, and a footlocker for the family. This was done
in blackout darkness with a shining flashlight in the back of a
dresser drawer open just a crack.

Other families had their own cars, so Naomi and I were
assigned to the Mission pickup truck with Kim Sung Soo,
the auto shop repairman driving. The pickup was already
loaded with extra suitcases. Naomi rode in the cab with Bonnie and Eloise and Lloyd and I sat on suitcases in the back.
We drove through the darkened city to pick up gas at the 8th
Army headquarters and then to the 121st Army hospital.

The families were to be evacuated by sea. The missionary
men helped the G.I.s load bedding, food and supplies onto
waiting trucks. A breakfast of fruit cocktail and chocolate
milk was supplied by the local Army unit. About nine o'clock
the Army convoy of buses carrying ladies and children headed for Inchon and a Norwegian freighter which lay at anchor
in Inchon harbour.

I said goodbye to Naomi and the children and they left
the hospital. I had to get back to the city and decide what to

do about the 33 Publishing House workers. A couple of missionaries from another denomination were heading back to Seoul in their jeep so I got a ride with them. They were headed for West Gate, so I got off in town and looked for transportation going to East Gate. Alas! No street cars were functioning, all buses were being used by the military and there were no taxis! Most transportation was being used to shuttle the wounded and dying from the battle lines. My stomach was growling from the effects of local bugs. As I looked across the street I saw an old man resting on a rickshaw. I asked the man if he could take me to Chung-ryang-ni, the location of the Mission. The old man coughed as he agreed for a price. I got in and we headed down the road to East Gate. I noticed the man had coughing spasms and was weak and his ribs were showing. Finally, we had to stop as the poor man had yet another coughing spell. I got out of the vehicle, gave the man a good fee, and told him to get some medicine.

I walked the rest of the way and arrived at a deserted, silent compound. The Press workers were standing in groups discussing the situation.

Naturally the news of war breaking out on the 38th Parallel would make them concerned. The Press did not have enough cash flow to pay them for the first two weeks of June, so I was very concerned about paying them for the month.

I had just come in through the Union office. On the way in I picked up a flyer with a picture of a butterfly that had been dropped by a Communist aircraft. In red letters the paper assured the people of Seoul to be calm: "The People's Republic of Chosen's Army will be in Seoul city in two days to liberate the Korean people from the American oppression and the corrupt government of Syngman Rhee."

Entering my office at the Press, I sat in my chair, trying to sort out my troubled thoughts. In a few moments Brother Chung Tae Hyuk brought more bad news. THE BANKS WERE CLOSED FOR THE DURATION OF THE WAR! This called for decisive action. We discussed the options and decided to call a general meeting of Press workers. The workers would have no way to provide food and transportation for their families in the event of sudden evacuation. The Publishing House officers met immediately with Korean Union leaders. Most institutions were struggling with the same problem.

We called a general meeting of all Press workers and presented the plan that the officers had suggested. We planned to share our assets with the workers. Due to wise planning of our treasurer, we had ten large 250-pound sacks of rice in storage, a good supply of box lumber that could be used for needed firewood, and the unbound signatures of books we had printed.

The staff kindly agreed to accept this plan, and a solemn prayer meeting closed the session. We did not know it then, but in the Providence of God, when the occupying Red Army questioned the Press workers, they learned that the people had not been paid for June. They kindly gave our workers rations. Praise the Lord for this blessing! The next day I was still adjusting the big #00 Miehle press when we got the news that the U.S. embassy would evacuate the men and that we were to be at Bando Hotel by 11 p.m.

Don Lee dropped by that evening as I was preparing to evacuate and asked me to go along with him to drive out to the College and help persuade his brother James to leave. James was busy meeting the faculty and arranging to evacuate the students. As we drove out past Tae-nung we caught up with the same cavalry we met the night before. They were using our school as a staging area. In all the commotion, one Korean soldier got trigger happy and shot his own horse. We could not stop to help and still meet our evacuation deadline.

At eleven p.m. we arrived at the center of the city. The air was throbbing with artillery and the mortars lit up the sky. We were assigned a room at the hotel and told that our evacuation would probably take place in the morning.

As I got ready for bed, I was amused to still be in greasy overalls since I'd been adjusting the big press that day with tools still in my pockets! Ambassador Mucio had just heard from the front line officers that the defense was crumbling. As I lay back on my bed, still in my overalls, I tried to doze off. Suddenly the sound of an approaching airplane pulled me back to the window. It was heading straight for the Bando

Hotel. I rolled out of bed onto the floor. Nothing happened! Turns out the plane was a friendly one (an L-19) being used by the officer in charge of directing the evacuation. He had flown directly from the front line of fighting and just dropped a note on the flat hotel roof for the Ambassador.

Evacuation morning, everybody was up early. A good breakfast of scrambled eggs and hash browns helped make the evacuees feel better. Leland Mitchell, of our Mission, was ready to use a fire axe to destroy the hotel's telephone exchange he was manning. Dr John Scharffenberg closed his emergency clinic at the hotel. Out on the hotel sidewalk, G.I.s were burning records and critical equipment with manganese flares. The buses painted orange were assembling in front, ready to take us to Kimpo airport.

Word went out that everyone was free to enter the PX across the road and help themselves. Some came out with new suits on and others had a row of new watches on both their arms. Most pockets were full of movie and 35-mm film. I just climbed into one bus and waited. Korean Army vehicles were running helter-skelter with bushes to camouflage the pots and bedding of their families as they fled south from the city.

Finally the order was given to head for Kimpo. We crossed the Han river and then it happened! A North Korean plane headed for the convoy, probably a T-16 training plane given to Russia. It came in low to strafe us, so the bus drivers slammed on the brakes by the curb. The driver of our bus jumped out and ran away. We all ducked to the floor as the plane roared by, his 50-mm gun rattling. I peeked out the window and saw an old man get hit in the shoulder and a little boy with him was hit in the face. What a gut-wrenching sight! Leland Mitchell jumped into the abandoned driver's seat and followed the convoy out of Yong-dong-po and headed for the airport.

We piled our baggage on the tarmac and lined up for a head count, about three hundred men and a few women. We were told that seven DC-6 planes would arrive to fly us to Fukuoka, Japan. One of our rescue planes had engine trouble and turned back to its base, so we could not take our suit-cases or foot lockers.

As we stood there we began the usual banter, teasing our Marine guards. Some had shotguns, pearl-handled six-shoot-ers and an assortment of military weapons. To the north of us, just ten miles away, the battle was raging on the Han river!

Suddenly, we were ordered to head for the basement of the old building. As we sat on some ammunition cases, we noticed that some cases were distributed around the rooms and wires were leading to the same! We were ordered back to the runway as our planes were coming in. We were star-tled at the unfamiliar jet engines as the U.S. Air Force F-80s circled overhead to form an umbrella as they picked off some of those pesky North Korean planes trying to bomb our air-port. A P-40 joined the jets to use its radar to keep track of the enemy. Several planes went down in flames.

As we adjusted our luggage, a shout went up that our planes were sighted. They came in ten-minute intervals, fly-ing low between the hills about one thousand feet above the deck. I was amused that the French Ambassador's wife was insisting on taking her two white poodles. "No dogs!" the of-ficer said. A missionary wanted to take his Chinese silk rug and his beloved German shepherd. "No" was the answer. One after another the planes landed and loaded passengers with their engines running.

We lined up to board our assigned plane and settled into our bucket seats in preparation for takeoff. Once airborne, a young man sat down beside Dr Meade Baldwin, seated next to me. He showed Meade his FBI badge and told him he would have to confiscate the 16-mm film he had taken during the evacuation. "The government will return the film later," he said politely.

As the last of the four-engine planes took off, a Communist plane slipped in and strafed the tail, but no damage was done. In a couple of hours we were circling the field in Fukuoka, Japan. We were taken to an Army barracks where we cleaned up for supper. After a good night rest, we were taken by train north to the island of Kyushu. The train waited in one station to let a troop train pass, loaded with advance units of the 25th Division. They were the Indian Head division and true to their name, the men cut their hair in Mohawk style and were singing war songs at the top of their voices. We did not know it then, but they were deployed south of Seoul to hold the line and hundreds paid the supreme price, as they were overwhelmed by the North Koreans in their Russian tanks.

After a long ride we pulled into Kobe station and were taken to the Sumo camp of Japan's famous wrestling team. My army cot was set right on the edge of the Sumo ring!

By this time we were all wondering where our families were staying. Dr Ralph Pearson had some Army contacts and in a few minutes he was able to call his wife and family. They had been taken to Karizawa, the Imperial vacation resort in the mountains northwest of Tokyo. This is where Emperor Hirohito took his family for rest. We had to make special arrangements to be released from the Kobe camp. Soon we were on a train heading for Karizawa.

When we arrived we checked into a hotel and looked for our families. What a welcome party we had! But, we had a surprise. The ladies had eaten their supper and were told to be ready to board a night train for Tokyo and evacuation to U.S.A.! The men scrambled to cancel their hotel reservations, buy tickets for the same train and head for Tokyo with their wives and children.

The commanding officer was not happy about all these men joining her group and holding babies and children in their laps. Fortunately for us, Elder Francis Millard, president of the Japan Union, had done his homework by preparing a letter from General Douglas MacArthur, allowing the Japan Mission to hold and house the Korean Union missionaries willing to stay in Japan.

Fourteen Korean Union missionary families were housed in the compound homes of the Japanese Mission. They were thankful for this hospitality.

Chapter 19

ENDLESS CONFLICT

With fourteen missionary families on board, the overnight train steamed into the Tokyo railway station from the royal resort of Karizawa. Frances Millard, Japan Union president, took out his handkerchief to wipe his sweaty brow as he checked his notes. It was hot and humid, past the 4th of July of 1950. This special military train was transporting hundreds of women and children fleeing from the hostilities on the Korean War. Millard was looking for a group of fourteen missionary families of the Korean Adventist Mission. As he walked along the line of cars, he finally recognized Elder Ernst Bahr, president of the Korean Union, and his wife. The missionaries were gathering in a group with their sleepy children. We were happy to see Elder Millard, for the Army captain in charge was unwilling to release the women and children to their husbands until she had further orders. Elder Millard showed her a letter from General Douglas MacArthur's office releasing the group to the Japan Mission leader.

Before long we were all at the Amanuma Mission compound, being given our housing assignments. The Far Eastern Division officers talked with the families and gave them options to return to their homeland or stay and wait for events to unfold. If they stayed, they could study the language or take new assignments in Asia. Those planning to stay could take a vacation at the Japan Union rest camp at Lake Nogiri for the summer.

Two delegates from the group were sent to Nogiri. They found an empty Japanese hotel and rented it for the summer. There was room enough for the four families who chose to stay.

Arrangements were made for the Tokyo hospital to send a truckload of springs, mattresses, linen and folding metal chairs. With a few dishes and kettles, the ladies were able to prepare delicious meals. These simple arrangements helped our families enjoy the summer vacation as we were debriefed from our harrowing ordeal.

Nogiri was not only a summer resort but the nearby town of Nagano was a famous winter resort. Daily our conversations drifted to the Korean conflict. We noticed that squadrons of B-29 bombers were making regular trips to the north. We did not know what was going on, so we pooled our cash and bought a Japanese radio. But, alas, it was an old tube set and the static distorted the news broadcasts.   Finally, we knew that we needed to get to a warmer area in Japan. So we sent Bob Mills and James Lee to Kobe. They came back with the good news that they had found a large four-story home that could accommodate four families. There was also a small cottage at the main gate where Mrs. Wangerin could live. There was even space for a schoolroom for the children and a small apartment for Helen Fessler, the teacher. Down in the basement there was room for a language school for the men. It was just right for the group who eventually called it KUMINEX (Korean Union Mission in Exile).

It was good news and everybody was ready to get settled. We had had a good rest and were now ready for a new life in Japan. About the end of August we packed up and boarded the train for Kobe. It was typhoon season in Japan and the train encountered heavy wind and pelting rain. The engineer had to stop the train many times. Slowly as we crept along we could see the village streets flooding and the cement tiles blowing off the roofs of the homes. The train did not have a diner, so we bought "bentos" from the vendors who came aboard at each station Finally our brave engineer got us to Kobe.

We busied ourselves getting settled. We bought some tiny but sturdy oak furniture for our apartments. But our apartment was too small for our family of five, so we went house hunting.

Renting in Japan or Korea can be a new experience. We found a little place, a two-story duplex, twelve feet wide and twenty-five feet deep. We paid Yen 10,000 (which was about

$275.00). The cleaners came in, washed all unpainted woodwork with trisodium, renewed all wallpaper and painted all walls and installed new straw on the tadami mats. I bought a Japanese saw, hammer and plane. Then I got some cedar 2x2s, mahogany plywood and built a little kitchenette under the steps to the second floor.

The toilet was something else! I bought a steel five-gallon bucket, cut the bottom out and welded a toilet seat to the other end. Then I welded tabs on the other end and screwed this device to the opening. That made an Asian commode!

Mrs. Theodora Wangerin was comfortably settled in her little cottage by the front gate. She was asked to set up a Korean language school for the missionaries who had recently arrived in the field It was known that in the suburbs of the city of Osaka about 20 miles from Kobe lived a population of about 230,000 Koreans. After scouting around, we found three young men who could teach the Korean language. They did not have knowledge on how to teach, but the missionaries helped them by writing their own syllabus. Mrs. Wangerin, a long-term missionary in Korea, gave them suggestions on how to teach conversation.

Elder C. W. Lee, who with his wife had worked several years in Korea, was elected as the new Union president.

Three men studied with the Korean language teachers. Each of them would set up a syllabus that would be appropriate for the kind of work he expected to do in Korea.

I wanted to work in ministerial and evangelistic lines. It was getting boring just mouthing diphthongs all day so the men made a plan to put their lessons into real-life situations by holding evangelistic meetings in the suburbs of Osaka, where most of the Korean people lived. They learned that half of the Korean population believed in democracy and the rest were Communists. This was a real challenge to the three men who planned to do the preaching. Mrs. Wangerin, our instructor, volunteered to translate for us and to help with the printing of literature. This project by these missionaries was blessed by the Lord. The attendance was good—no riots—and in two years 40 people were baptized. The Japan

Mission helped provide funds to build a church and send a pastor for this new congregation.

The war in Korea had degenerated to a last-ditch stand. United Nations troops that had joined the American divisions were scattered along the Naktong river in the south and had been pushed to the southeast sector of Korea, just 100 miles from the sea!

Something extraordinary was to happen! While the North Korean commanders were preparing their divisions for a final thrust to the sea, General Douglas MacArthur secretly prepared a massive invasion armada ready to do the impossible! ATTACK AND OUTFLANK NORTH KOREA'S DIVISIONS AT THE IMPORTANT HARBOUR OF INCHON! In August and September of 1950, waves of B-29 bombers and squadrons of fighters hit the Communist troops behind the lines on the Naktong river. Then suddenly by surprise, on September 15, a mighty Navy landed the Marines on the island of Wolmi in Inchon harbour. By the twenty-sixth, the troops were in Seoul. After weeks of fighting, 128,000 Communist prisoners were inside the prison camps of Ko Jae island!

After the U.N. troops stabilized the situation on the Korean peninsula, the missionary men were allowed to return and work in the southern sector of the country. Some headquartered in Pusan and others worked in Seoul. In 1951 I organized an evangelistic team and stayed with the men in the Pusan house and used many means of travel.

One of my first jobs was to assist Dr. Rue as he arranged for an L.S.T. transport to move several hundred Adventist workers and members of other denominations. They were headed for Sung San Po, on the island of Cheju.

The situation in Pusan was critical. Our church was trying to help hundreds of believers who were stranded by the war. As I worshipped with our people, I was planning to call four young men to travel with me to encourage the people in the country to trust in the Lord. One Sabbath while singing with the congregation, I heard a young man singing tenor. I contacted him and Yu Chon Sik became part of our quartet. Later Choi Hui Man and Pak Sin Ho were called. We now had our quartet from Sahmyook College. I sang the bass

Places Visited During and After the War

Working with an evangelistic team, George shakes hands wtih our leading evangelist and speaker, Elder Woo Pill Won.

part. The mission of our team was to hold revival meetings in the churches and sing the praises of God. This would comfort the church suffering the traumas of war.

Elder Im Sung Won was called to be our preaching evangelist. At first we traveled by bus, train and motor launch which was hard work, for we had to carry all our equipment and supplies by hand.

Beginning at Kangnung on the east coast, we stayed at the home of the chief of police whose wife was a church member. It was a nice home. Our hostess made all kinds of preparations to entertain the team. She even made special brocade quilts for the guests and prepared wonderful meals. I got a private bedroom and servants fired up the ondol (floor heater) so that when I went to bed the silk floss quilt and the hot floor almost roasted me! I was sweating in no time and got up to grope around to find a cooler spot. The closet had a wooden floor, so I retreated there!

The team completed their work in Kangnung and took the bus down the coast to a fishing village named Chukpyunni, where there was one Adventist family. The leader had arranged to use a large fish warehouse for an auditorium. They moved the great bales of dried fish. There were no seats so the people sat on balsawood floats left over by the Navy. At one end of the building stood sixteen empty oil drums. Planks over the top of these made it a platform. One drum became the pulpit. Three empty apple boxes made steps up to this rustic platform.

Elder Im Sung Won, a North Korean was the preacher. He had come down from North Korea between the fighting. (He carried his young son on his back as he climbed over the tangled superstructure of the bombed bridge across the Imjin river.) While staying with us he had been elected by the laymen of the church to lead out in the north territory, so he visited headquarters in Seoul. Our team remembers the nightmares he had from this trauma.

Just before the meetings began our team passed out handbills all over town and put up posters advertising the meetings. One day an elderly grandma saw our poster on a power pole. She had come down from the hills to attend "chang-nal" (market day). (At that time Korean peasants brought their goods for sale every fifth day of the week). She was so interested in the meeting that she came to the house to inquire and found a place to stay. She was a Buddhist but full of questions in her searching for truth. The Communists had forced her to cook rice and prepare meals for them, finishing off everything she had. She prayed for protection but this mistreatment continued. She asked for a Bible and I gave Grandma my own Korean Bible.

On the opening night Grandma was there in that dark warehouse hall, lit by only a couple of 60-watt bulbs. Grandma was fascinated by a drawing on the wall behind the pulpit of Jesus sitting on a bright cloud, holding a sickle in one hand and a trumpet in the other. Slowly, with her eyes on the picture, she walked up to the rostrum and climbed the steps. A deacon was going to stop her, but I motioned for him to let her alone. Standing behind the pulpit and facing the picture of Jesus, King of Kings, she reverently put her hands together and clapped, just like she was used to when worshiping the image of Buddha.

While we were holding these meetings we heard that the Communist guerrillas had staged a raid in a village south of Chukpyun. In this raid they had mistreated a U.N. employee and a missionary. We discussed these forebodings and decided to stay, and the Lord protected us.

At that time we did not see the results of our meetings in this fishermen's village, but in the fall of 1997 Naomi and I, our daughter Eloise and her husband, Todd Murdoch, were traveling south to visit the city of Kyung-ju. We stopped at Chuk-pyun and found a beautiful new town with high-rise buildings and modern roads. We walked into the market place to buy some hot rice cakes called "dueck." I asked the lady if there were any Christian sales people around. She said, "Right there" and pointed to a lady selling dried seaweed. I saw her reading "The Desire of Ages." I asked her if she attended an Adventist church and she said, "Yes." Over fifty members are attending and she invited us to visit the pastor and her church.

Back to 1952—war was still raging. We packed and said goodbye to the people at Chuk-pyun. In our farewell prayer we asked that the Lord bless our friend—-Grandma from the hills.

Our traveling team stood by the roadside waiting for the express bus that was due to stop. In those days of war economy, buses were built of steel flattened from drums, very buslike, mounted on a military 2 ½ ton GMC truck. We saw one careening down the road, loaded inside with people. We had to shove hard to get in and the kind people offered me a seat on a box of apples.

We rattled down the washboard road past mile after weary mile of emerald green rice fields ripening in the fall sunshine. Peeking through the screen of peasants' bodies, I spied a Korean Army checkpoint! I thought, "Oh, oh! Here goes another delay." Sure enough, the M.P. blew his whistle. Then he walked around the bus inspecting the tires. THEY WERE ALL STAMPED WITH "ROK" (REPUBLIC OF KOREA ARMY). He stepped up to the door of the bus and shouted, "All passengers must get off this bus. We are taking all the stolen tires off." We were way out in the country with no lodging for miles.

As I got off the bus I reached out my hand and greeted the M.P. in Korea. Respectfully I asked to talk to the sergeant. We stepped to one side and I asked that he exempt this bus from seizure because we had an important appointment for meetings in Pohang and needed to make connection on to Pusan. The soldier was surprised to hear a foreigner speak Korean. Then he smiled. "Yes, we will excuse this one bus." Relieved we all climbed back in. Jokingly I announced, "This is now the Yang-ko-begi Kuephaeng" (the long-nosed express). This brought peals of laughter from the peasant passengers.

The ancient west coast hamlet of Hong Sung, like many ancient cities of Korea, was protected by a wall and large gates. When the North Korean Communist troops invaded the town, the young men of Hong Sung put up a desperate battle, using farm implements against guns and mortars. Two hundred and eighty men died and are buried a mile from town in a mound about fifty feet high. We had meetings here in the Korean Army veterans' hall. We preached the gospel and the quartet sang gospel songs to a standing-room-only audience. I was deeply moved by the story of twenty widows of the men who were lying in that huge grave. They were members and in desperate need of food and clothing for their families. Our local church members were helping, but they were overwhelmed by the burden.

In 1953, when we were on furlough in California, I shared the story of the Hong Sung widows with the members of a church in the California foothills. After the worship service a lady spoke to me. She was a World War II widow from Holland who had immigrated to the U.S. to work as a maid and caregiver. Her employer had passed away and left a considerable part of the estate to her. She gave me a check for $1,000.00 to buy sewing machines for the Korean widows to earn a living. We bought ten machines and delivered them. One of them took up tailoring and set up shop on the island of An Myun. She tailored men's suits and also raised up a church on that island!

To improve our travel situation, our Mission mechanic, Kim Sung Soo, bought a jeep engine from the U.S. Embassy. He scrounged other parts and cobbled together a jeep for the team and painted it a bright sky blue. On the front panel below the windshield were lettered the words, "Adventist Mission" with a drawing of a Bible and a torch. "Old Betsy" served us faithfully for thousands of miles.

We always kept new tires on our jeep and an ammunition box full of spark plugs and spare parts. One day the team was traveling through the pine forest of the Chiri mountains in south central Kyungsan province. Suddenly, the jeep lurched to the side of the road. As the driver slammed on the brakes, we slid right up to a big pine tree just off the road. Sliding under the front end, we found that the main bolt on the steering bar had fallen off. We walked back down the road, found the bolt, and installed it again. That called for a prayer of gratitude to God.

We arrived in Dong Hae on market day. All around us was evidence of a terrible battle. Trees on the hill near us were stripped of leaves, the ground was plowed by mortar shells and the houses were in shambles. Our quartet climbed onto a pile of rubble and began singing "Jesus, Keep Me Near the Cross." People gathered round to hear this close harmony. One old man, probably a Christian, mouthed the words and soon tears rolled down his cheeks. We invited the listeners to the meetings to hear more music. We sang to the church members, to evangelistic audiences and to high school gatherings. One day we even stopped by a middle school and sang to the boys, closing with a short encouraging talk. Our quartet became ambassadors of hope in a deadly war.

One Sunday I was driving south alone when I came upon a company of sixteen American tanks parked in tight formation in a compound. I stopped to talk to the commander and was invited to hold a Sunday religious service for the men who were heading out shortly for the front lines of the battle. Sitting on the turret of a tank, I presented a message of encouragement and hope. I offered a prayer that God would protect them and keep them through the day.

While the team was holding meetings in Hong Sung, Elder Im, our speaker, had an appointment to meet in Seoul city. Brother Kim Sung Nei, our driver, took Elder Im to Seoul. On the way back, a Korean M.P. stopped him, confiscated the jeep and put Kim in a holding jail. Kim sent word that he needed help. At that time, I was having trouble sleeping because of stomach pains, but I needed to help our driver. So I stirred up a hot drink, climbed on a bus and headed for Chun-an. As the bus drove down the road, I spotted the jeep driving south with a grinning M.P. at the wheel. So I got off the bus and flagged down the jeep. If I hadn't we probably would never have seen it again.

Chun-an (Heavenly Peace) was a key town on the road to Seoul. We secured the town hall for our meetings. The war had ravaged the place, leaving no doors or windows.

But the basement jail was quite secure and we were treated to the sound of prisoners begging for cigarettes, wanting to communicate with somebody. Heavy rice sacks were laid on the cement floor for seating. Our quartet music soothed the sad hearts of the people who were traumatized by the awful war conditions. When we sang "When Peace Like a

River Attendeth My Soul," their hearts were healed. One of the prisoners in the basement listened to the sermons by pressing his ear to the bars. Our local laymen gave him Bible studies and later, when he was released, he came to church.

The team stayed at the home of the church elder, Brother and Sister Hur Suk. His wife was a good cook, but the war caused all kinds of shortages. Most people had lost their homes and all possessions. They gave me the best room in the house, and the lady brought my meals to the room on a separate tray, according to the treatment of a guest in Korean tradition. I protested to the man of the house, saying I wanted to eat with the rest of the family. So I joined the family around the big pot of mixed vegetables and rice ("peebin-pap"). I was still learning the Korean language and found mealtimes a good place to practice.

Today there is a church in Chon An and a food factory organized by the Australian Sanitarium Foods Industry. They are producing meat substitutes and soy milk sold in health food stores around the world.

In early 1953 our team visited Masan to hold meetings in a tent pitched by the Mission. Elder Woo Pil Won was the speaker. We were opposed by the local Protestant leaders. Not long after our meetings, the local police tried to suppress a riot by high school students. A policeman made the mistake of shooting a canister of tear gas at a student. The missile hit a boy in the eye and killed him. The police tried to cover up the mistake by taking the body into the police station, putting weights on the body and dumping it into the ocean. In a couple of days the body floated and this incident triggered the student riots that ended in toppling President Syngman Rhee's government.

I will never forget the day when the college and high school students took control of the streets of Seoul. I was assigned to drive the Mission pickup to Inchon and meet a new doctor and his wife who had come by ship to work in Pusan hospital. I was on my way back to the Mission and was crossing the Han river bridge when a caravan of rioting students were headed south. The advance vehicle was a white police jeep full of students singing victory songs and brandishing baseball bats. The truck load of screaming youth were pointing at our truck. A college student with a bat in his hand came running over towards us. As he came near, I shouted that we were missionaries. The student shouted back to the group, "Sung-gyo-sa" (Missionary). Right at that moment a siren sounded and an American M.P. pulled up and ordered me to follow him. We turned around and quickly retreated. The M.P. advised us to bypass the city to get back to the Mission compound.

The political situation in Korea was tense as the students continued to make demands against political corruption. They did bring order to the cities and temporarily cleaned up the mess. Political unrest continued for nine more months.

On my way to Inchon for our next meetings, I was stopped in Yong-dong-po by a Korean C.I.D. who advised me that conditions were not good for any kind of meeting. We cancelled it. I stood by the railway track watching the students confronting the police.

While this was going on, a group of Adventist ministers decided to visit Mr. Chung, the interim president. He was a Presbyterian layman who was being bitterly criticized from all sides. We felt sorry for him and decided to visit his office, have prayer with him and let him know that all Christians were praying for him. During the visit, with tears in his eyes, he thanked us for praying for him and he asked that we pray for his country.

We had one problem—getting decent food when traveling although the food was always excellent at our church members' homes. I picked up an intestinal problem that caused sleeplessness. The boys suggested that I needed chicken soup. It did help a little but I decided to drive to Seoul and get professional treatment from the Sanitarium. Miss Irene Robson took charge, ordering hydrotherapy and vitamin B shots. In less than a week I was feeling good again and thanked the Lord for the medical treatments at a Christian hospital.

It was time for me to fly back to my family in Yokohama and help them pack up for our much needed furlough in California.

Chapter 20

POST-WAR SERVICE

Korea was devastated by the war and thousands of military and civilian lives were lost. City after city had been leveled, peoples' homes had been pounded to rubble, but their spirit had not been destroyed. Like a wounded animal struggling to get on its feet, the people of the "Land of Morning Calm" rose up again to courageously rebuild their society. It took a miracle of God's grace to inspire the thousands of stouthearted people to rebuild and develop their country into the industrial nation that South Korea is today.

In May, 1954, Naomi and I stood at the very center of downtown Seoul. We were standing on a pile of rubble in front of what had been the Bank of Korea. Right before us was a gaping hole with steps going down to a basement. Hearing a noise, we were surprised to see two little Korean urchins come out of the hole and clamber up to the top of the steps. One hesitated, the other ran off to look for a scrap of food in someone's garbage! Orphans are the "lost generation" of their brave country. Even today, hundreds of war orphans are searching for lost loved ones.

Naomi and I are so happy that God gave our family the opportunity to return to post-war Korea to help our beloved Korean friends pick up the shards of war and rebuild their families and a new nation.

Prior to the war, the expanding Korean Union Mission had needed more pastors, so the Mission committee voted to establish the Korean Union Seminary. The Lord helped the Mission purchase 190 acres of prime land from the Royal Household of South Korea. It was covered with pine forests and a mix of azalea bushes, rhododendron and forsythia. Part of the land was connected to the range of hills that came down from Uijunbu and ends at the prominent granite Peak "Puramsan."

Elder James Lee and Elder Lee Yu Sik, along with other Mission leaders, developed plans to establish a college where Adventist youth could receive training for service in God's church in Korea.

Through James's good connections with the U.S. Corps of Engineers, they agreed to build a reservoir on the hill behind the school. At the same time they excavated an area where granite blocks could be quarried to use in building some of the dormitories and classroom buildings. Lee Mitchell, Mission builder, supervised the repair of Mission homes, offices and the Seoul Sanitarium and Hospital. Eventually he worked full time building the new Sahmyook campus. This college project was moving ahead on schedule until June 25, 1950. Part of their work was destroyed by the war that raged from June 1950 to the summer of 1953.

With the end of the war, the Mission was able to begin rebuilding the school. James Lee's brother Donald was called to be president of the new school. I was asked to help train young people to become workers in the Adventist churches— focusing on the Bible/Ministerial training.

In the summer of 1954, Dr. Donald S. Lee and his wife Blanche and two daughters, Cheryle and Sandra, moved into the president's home on campus. He assembled his faculty and met around a table, under the pine trees of the new campus. They opened the book "Education" and made plans for the new year by following the advice of the Lord through Ellen White's pen. The overall plan was based on the work-study principle. Each teacher was assigned a work project and would put in at least four hours per week in leading a group of ten students to work on rebuilding the college.

I was assigned a group of fine young men and trained them to paint the buildings in an organized and neat way. I wrote to my Uncle Paul in Napa, California, and requested a supply of tools. Paul sent a good set of brushes and putty knives as well as white painters' overalls and painters' caps. WHAT A TEAM WE MADE! The boys painted each building as soon as the carpentry work was finished. We organized a painters' chorus and they sang as we painted together, "I've Been Workin' on the Railroad."

My greatest challenge was teaching in the Korean language. The students were very troubled about the examinations they would get after listening to the lectures in a mixture of English and broken Korean. I told them not to worry. We had produced a syllabus in Korean for every class, and the examinations were based on the syllabus only.

That first year we spent hours with a translator and more hours over the grading of the lessons. I taught "Life and Teachings of Jesus," "Public and Personal Evangelism," "English As A Second Language," "Ministerial Graphics," and "Elementary Art."

We worked alongside the ministerial students in summer field schools as they applied the principles taught in class. The school and Union ministerial department provided funds to hold public meetings in nearby "Anyang" and street meetings in the inner city of Seoul.

The students will never forget their summer class on Yokchi Do, an island off the coast of South Korea. We assembled a group of six or eight students to work with an evangelist and travel by train and bus to the coastal town of Tong-yong. We were met at the wharf by Pastor Lee Yung Jim who helped us load our luggage onto a small diesel launch. As we settled down for the trip, they speculated excitedly in anticipation as to what it was going to be like on an island where people had never seen a Christian program or a white man before. As the launch encountered larger waves, the team grew silent. Soon some were leaning over the railing—"feeding the fish!"

A group of local islanders met us and led us to an empty house which was to be our "hotel." We brought our own bedding and some pots and pans. The two young ladies who were taking the Bible Worker's course prepared meals for the group. The rest of the team scurried off to prepare the hall (a former Japanese school). We borrowed an old electric generator. The team had prepared handbills to advertise the meetings so we organized an advertising team and started visiting house to house. We came to the first home and in accordance with Korean custom called out, "Is anyone home?" The lady of the house came to the door, gasped and ran back into her house. The islanders were unaccustomed to seeing a white man, so I had to linger in the background as the students made the invitation to attend the meetings.

The group enjoyed the fellowship as we worked together on this new phase of evangelism on this remote Korean island. One day at dinner we were playing a game of "Guess What the Ladies Put in the Vegetable Soup?" Each person was naming off some veggies. When it was my turn I said "*kamja*" (potatoes) and "*Pah*" (onions), then "*menuri*" (daughter-in-law). I had mispronounced the word for "celery" which is "*minari*". This brought hearty laughter. From that time on the famous missionary joke was Pastor Munson ate "daughter-in-law" soup at Yokchi Do.

In the evening, people came to the meetings from all over the island. Each carried a candle in a paper shade or a kerosene lantern. They enjoyed the preaching and the slides. On the last night, while Elder Pang Nei Hyun was offering the benediction, he was repeating the words of the Bible text, "Babylon is fallen, is fallen," when suddenly there was a loud crash, and the generator stopped! In the darkness all was pandemonium with people shouting, some shoving the sliding windows until they popped out onto the ground. When someone finally turned on a flashlight, the crowd was milling around, trying to find their rubber shoes. We discovered the floor of the building had collapsed two feet to the ground.

When they finally found their shoes, they left for home. The team members were apologetic and concerned about two pregnant ladies in the group, but no one was hurt. The building was repaired and later a worker returned to the island and raised up a church.

The first post-war class of college students became strong workers who led out in a time of solid church growth. There were thirty-five young men and women in that first graduation class. Two of then, Chun Pyung Duk and Kim Tong Joon, did so well that the Far Eastern Division called them to serve in the Division headquarters at Singapore. Elder Chun became president of the Division and Elder Kim was the secretary. They both learned to speak English well and served with honor. Another young man, Pai Suk Won, came to us with prior training and interest in radio and TV technology.

Brother Pai was my secretary while attending school. He knew English well enough to help translate classroom material and prepare class documents.

Every Sabbath afternoon this first class joined a group of students who helped carry out the mission of their school. They fanned out into the local villages to hold branch Sabbath Schools, children's meetings and evangelistic programs. The evangelism class held meetings in local villages. Our GMC panel truck had a platform on the roof from where they could project movies or show slide programs.

During the three years I was teaching at Sahmyook College, the students raised up branch Sabbath Schools and companies of believers. Don Lee encouraged the faculty members to make it a hands-on program just as Ellen White suggested in the book "Evangelism." Later, we held on-location classes for the ministerial students during larger campaigns. Ministers from the local churches were involved.

As other missionary families joined the teaching staff at Sahmyook, the Mission built a school house from parts of a military Quonset hut and hired Miss Shafer to educate their children, Grades 1-8. Part of the education was to caution the children about handling hand grenades or rockets and other weapons they might find on the grounds. Many Korean children died playing with ordnance (rockets, hand grenades, land mines, artillery shells, etc.) left over from the war. Thankfully, no missionaries' children were hurt.

In the summer of 1958 we moved our family to a two-story home on the hospital grounds. I was given a new assignment—to direct the Voice of Prophecy Bible Correspondence School, and to build a radio and television ministry. My office was on the second story of the Press building. We assembled a fine team of workers. The younger members had just finished studies at Sahmyook College. Pai Suk Won was called to be in charge of the radio and television recording. His first assignment was to build a recording studio to prepare programs for broadcast on national radio stations.

Elder Pak Won Sil directed the VOP Bible Correspondence School. We praised the Lord for sending 120,000 Bible school students. Many of these Bible Correspondence students were

Our radio and television personnel, including radio speaker, announcer, Bible School director, workers, engineers, and secretaries. What a wonderful gospel team!

50 Souls Were Baptized

전도대강연회장

Two quonset huts were put together to hold about 1,800 people.

prisoners. Our VOP staff held graduation ceremonies in many prisons all over Korea. Nine hundred prisoners finished the course in the Seoul National Prison alone.

In 1960, I was asked to lead out in the Ministerial department of the Union. The first evangelistic campaign was held in Chegi-dong, a suburb of Seoul city. The Union provided the funds to erect a temporary hall where these meetings could be held. We used two large Quonset buildings and raised them up on wooden frames to make a hall large enough to seat 2,000 people.

We arranged with the College to pitch a tent next to the hall for our ministerial students to live in and get hands-on training. They led out in the children's meetings. From the first night, the hall was packed and the children's area sounded like a rookery of hundreds of sparrows! The next night our students organized the program and kept the children under control. (They put one college student in charge of twenty boys or girls.) They entered the hall in an orderly way and kept the program fast-moving and interesting.

To promote our health message, Naomi organized a vegetarian cooking class for the ladies. The class was successful with fifty ladies attending that first class. Naomi, with a college student interpreting, helped the people understand the concern the Lord has for the health of all of His children.

The Korean Union purchased a supply of used squad tents which were repaired and used by orphanages, churches and other gatherings. From these the Union constructed larger tents for use in the evangelistic program of the Missions. In 1963 and 1964 we held large meetings in the major cities of Korea. The Southeast Mission pitched their tent in the city of Taegu where Elder Woo Pil Won, the Union evangelist, preached. He moved on to Taejon and Chegi-dong resulting in nearly 50 baptisms. The largest tent that the Southwest Mission built was in Kwangju. That tent was pitched over a wooden frame where more than 2,000 people came to meet. The baptism was held in the local municipal swimming pool. Elder Woo held the meetings and was very tired after baptizing over 70. Elder C. H. Davis, Union president, planned to come down from Seoul to observe our evangelistic work. He told Naomi to accompany him by train to Kwang-ju. Surprised, she reminded him she had to care for the children at home. He told her to get a baby sitter: "Let's surprise your husband." When I met the taxi to greet Elder Davis, I was speechless to see Naomi.

Before 1964, a large city-wide evangelistic effort had not been attempted in the city of Seoul. We decided to hold just such a meeting in the Sam Ill High School auditorium. This was located next to the government center in Seoul. The planning had begun a year earlier. Brother Paeng Yong Kun, a very dedicated young worker, was my managing associate. During the year leading up to these meetings we held special revivals. Our first revival and promotional program began with a mountain retreat with sixty of the elders from every church within the metropolitan area. Brother Paeng prepared a booklet outlining all the plans that had been decided by the evangelism committee.

The team arrived at the Protestant Retreat Center on Sam Gak Mountain on a Thursday evening. Friday morning. Brother Paeng Yong Kun and I presented the plan concept by concept. There were to be five revivals, a 100-voice choir, the Voice of Prophecy quartet and 150 laymen who did the visitation and Bible work. There would be three booths in the hall, a small clinic, a VOP booth, and a cafeteria to feed the team. We planned a large city-wide rally in the largest hall available in Seoul. Just two days before the meetings, an all-night prayer vigil was to be held. Every church would sponsor special prayer groups to pray for God's blessings.

The meetings were to be advertised by newspaper, with large banners over the major streets near the Sam Ill High School and 400,000 handbills.

The sixty churches sponsoring the campaign were ready. Prayer groups met in homes and churches. We visited one group that met in a local park and met forty devoted ladies kneeling on rice-straw sacks on the ground. These were the wives and daughters of non-Adventist husbands and fathers. (Seven of their husbands came to the meetings and were baptized.) Praise the Lord for this result.

The sixty elders assembled at Sam Gak mountain agreed that the plans were good but they were not ready to vote for

Hundreds attended the meetings and responded to appeals.

172 baptisms in Seoul Olympic swimming pool

Brother You Chun Sik, translator

a financial budget of W180,000.00 for this evangelistic effort. They tabled the vote and went on with the spiritual revival program. They thought it was too large a sum of money.

Friday evening they had a big bonfire in the yard and the group sat around this blazing fire as I (who was to be the campaign speaker) talked about Pentecost and the "Fire of the Spirit." As I closed my appeal I used the "valley of dry bones" illustration found in Ezekiel 37. I appealed to the leaders to pray that the city churches would come to life and that God would allow the wind of the Holy Spirit to blow on the city of Seoul, and revive the membership of the churches and bring them back to spiritual life.

Sunday morning the sun rose on a beautiful day. The group gathered and the elders' spokesman stood and said that they were ready to vote a better budget for the campaign. That budget was set at W220,000.00. Indeed, the Spirit of God was with them and they went home enthusiastic about the whole program. (When the campaign was over, after four weeks, the team had collected W280,000.00.)

The Sabbath before the meetings, a rally was held in the largest hall in the city, attended by over 3,000 church members who were helping in the campaign. They distributed 350,000 handbills to the members who were encouraged to pass them out to friends and neighbors as they returned home.

Sabbath evening, the night before the meetings began, 500 members from the many churches in Seoul came to the hall and took part in the all-night prayer vigil. They also organized a pulpit prayer group of men and women who met in the room beside the platform to pray for the speaker and the program.

God blessed these meetings. Night after night men and women came forward to answer the call to accept Jesus as their Saviour. One evening two men came down and wanted to talk to me. They were concerned about their homosexual habits. I was shocked as they shared their story! I had never encountered this problem before and did some study in order to help the men.

A large group of laymen were given books of bus tickets. They visited house to house in the community near the high school. In many cases they brought the people to the meetings.

One of the Adventist ladies found a woman ready to commit suicide because her husband had left her. She prayed for her and brought her to the meetings every night. This lady joined the group of 172 people Elder Woo Pill Won had prepared for baptism. Later, 50 more were added to the churches.

This campaign took place after the student uprising that toppled the Syngman Rhee regime. In 1965 plans were made to hold special meetings for the youth of Seoul. Drugs, liquor and politics were big issues with the university students. The evangelism committee decided to hold meetings for the youth and appeal to the need to solve some of their troubles.

The Korean Union Mission wanted to establish an evangelistic center in the inner city. They decided to sign a rental contract with the Chongro Wedding Center. It was called a *"Chunsay."* The church would give the Wedding Center a payment of US$12,000.00 and we would be given the key and the right to use any of the seven halls for evangelistic meetings. We also were allowed to put up our own signs. We could use the facility as long as we wished to.

We chose the hall that seated four hundred people which had a good stage with a piano and visual aid equipment. Since Korean people do not hold weddings at night, this very nice hall could be used every night.

Brother Paeng used good strategy in planning for the program. First, we bought eight hundred Bibles which were handed out to the youth to use for the meetings and then they were collected at the door. We used a Bible-marking plan, and the students from Sahmyook College helped with the distribution and use of the Bibles.

A very modern, attractive handbill was printed with the title "Solving the Problems of Modern Youth." Hundreds of Adventist university students passed these out to the students that were entering the gates of most of the 27 universities in Seoul. We discussed the abuse of alcohol and tobacco and other social problems that trouble youth.

Even though spring was the youth's usual season for fighting the police in the streets, yet they packed the hall twice every evening (at six and again at eight). Most of the youth carried bags for their books. When they were handed a Bible, they paid good attention.

The whole program was geared for youth. I spoke in English and Brother Chung translated. Each program lasted one hour. Beginning with a choir of thirty college students, we then offered a short meaningful prayer and asked the audience to open their Bibles. The sermon was illustrated in Korean on a blackboard and flash cards.

We concluded with an appeal, inviting those who wished for spiritual guidance to join counselors who were either ministers, psychologists or physicians. These professionals were seated at tables marked with cards, indicating the particular help desired. Praise the Lord for the wonderful group of seventy young people who joined the baptismal class and were baptized. They were taken to our Adventist college and introduced to a more Christian lifestyle.

As we traveled all over Korea, we became aware of the needs of people groups the church was not reaching. One group we visited in South Kyung-san province was Ha-Dong, a leprosarium run by a layman. They had a very poor clinic to care for the daily medical needs of more than twenty patients. We appealed to the Seoul Sanitarium to send instruments and medical supplies to stock their clinic. An Adventist minister from North Korea, who had long been separated from his wife and his children by the Korean war, decided to be the shepherd of these lepers in South Korea.

As our evangelistic work took us to many areas, we would look up leprosariums and hold meetings, providing music for them and showing them Bible and nature movies. Many of them had never seen movies because, just like ancient times, lepers could not enter a hall where other people were gathered. Society did not know that leprosy can be controlled with medication.

Another group of neglected people were the orphans of the Korean war. We took an interest in working for orphans and by promoting the work done by of helping those who ran homes for these children. At Christmas time, Naomi and I encouraged our children to hold a Christmas program for the orphans. They prepared a small Christmas gift, such as warm socks or fruit for each child. That was lots of fun!

Right after the Korean war, about the fall of 1953, George talked to some Mission presidents about providing medical care for the thousands of homeless families huddled in little shacks on the outskirts of the cities of Korea. Many of these shanty towns were next to the military camps of the United Nations armies. One such city was Chun-ju, a provincial capital. The people went to the garbage dumps of these military camps and scrounged for scrap lumber, food, cardboard boxes, cans and bottles. They could eke out an existence on these meager supplies but they did not have medical care for when a baby was born or when a member of the family had a bad cold or pneumonia. They would try herbal medications, but there was sickness everywhere.

Elder Shin Chong Kyun volunteered to hire a Mission nurse with midwife credentials to hold clinics in town. Nurse Ellen Park volunteered to do this work so they bought a lady's bicycle which helped her get to the mothers who needed a midwife right now! Even in the middle of the night,

After the baby was born, she instructed the new mother on how to bathe her child, give it vitamins and soy milk powder and a bottle for milk. Her patients appreciated her help, but others who saw this young lady riding a bike in the wee hours of the night began to gossip. Soon the police were raising questions. Ellen wrote to me for help. I responded by driving to Chon-ju. I told Nurse Ellen to put on her uniform and cap and join me in visiting the mayor of the city. We were received graciously and I asked the mayor if he was acquainted with the work Nurse Ellen was doing for the refugees. We told him about the midwifery work, the health instructions for the people and the welfare food Nurse Ellen was distributing to the needy families. We also reminded him that the Seoul Sanitarium had equipped a clinic in town with a bed, cabinets, medical supplies and instruments for the clinic. Also, this clinic was serving the people every morning from 10:00 a.m. to 6:00 p.m. and that every day a line of people came to be treated.

Needless to say, the mayor was very pleased that this was being done for his people. Not only did he approve of Nurse Ellen's work, but he asked her to prepare health talks for the people to be broadcast every morning at 6:00 a.m.! In those days the government had set up a communication system which brought news and government information to each home by wire. The Lord blessed the program and later Nurse Ellen was broadcasting the Voice of Prophecy programs daily. When more funds were received, the local Mission hired another Sanitarium nurse to work with her. Today they have well equipped clinics, administered by trained doctors with a good community health program in the local Conferences. This follows the advice given years ago by Ellen G White.

Another people group that has not been reached are the thousands of Korean people who live on hundreds of islands that surround the Korean peninsula. One evening, while talking to an Adventist soldier, I shared my concern about these neglected island mission fields. I told him of my visits to some of these islands. The islanders were poor fishermen and subsistence farmers, I said, "If we only had a couple of diesel launches we could take medical people out to the islands and treat their diseases." The soldier, we'll call him Ron, said, "How much would you need to get this project started?" I figured on a scrap of paper and came up with the figure—$5,000.00. A few weeks later this soldier came back with a check for that very amount. We talked with the presidents of three Missions and asked them how this project would appear to their committees. They were enthusiastic. Elder Lee Yong Jin, of the Southeast Mission, offered to begin a pilot project with the first launch, a fishing boat with a diesel engine. They organized a team of Pusan hospital medical people and a couple of interns, brought along a public address system and packed up the needed medical supplies and instruments.

A group of interested members from the Dong Nei church gathered at the fishing wharf to dedicate the launch, naming it "The Southern Light." The Mission president explained the mission of the launch. This was to be a medical aid trip, but they would give health lectures and Bible studies as well. After special prayer for this mission, the captain started the engine and soon they waved goodbye to a happy group of "island" missionaries. An hour later, the captain ran the boat up on the sandy beach of a small island and the team set up their clinic. The P.A. system was used to call the islanders to the side of the launch where the medical team worked. That evening they brought out the screen and projector, the health lecture and the Daniel 2 film, "Birth of a New World" were shown. The islanders were very interested and the national workers were learning how to reach the island people.

The Mission presidents were pleased to hear about this pilot program, so we bought two more launches, and the Missions continued this successful new form of evangelism. This work continued until two of the boats were wrecked in the typhoon of 1964 and the third boat was stolen. Brother Yun Chi Seun, a lay evangelist was sent to An Myun island to plant several churches. In 1966 there were twelve churches and one grade school on that island. Later, that school became a junior academy. It is only by the grace of God and the faithful work of His people that the islands heard of Jesus and His love.

The island of Che-ju has an interesting history. Most men living on the island are fishermen. Down through the years typhoons have raced through the straits between Japan and Korea. Many times these fishermen were caught in them, never to come home. So many widows were left to lead out in the Che-ju community, the government became matriarchal.

About 1963 we visited the island of Che-ju, and held evangelistic meetings. I met an elderly woman who had become an Adventist Christian back in the 1930s when Japan was in power. She had been faithful in setting aside her tithes and offerings but had not known how to turn over her tithes to the Mission because there was no church in her area. So she hid her offerings under a floor board of her house. When I visited her, she was ninety-five years old and wanted to turn over her money to the Mission. I was surprised to find so many antique Japanese coins in her money.

Each year the Missions sponsored four evangelistic campaigns which kept our teams busy. One effort was scheduled for Wonju. The Mission did not have the funds to build a canvas tent, so they suggested that the ladies of the community service of the church sewed up a lot of white flour sacks and used this to cover a light wooden frame. It made a beautiful white tent.

Naomi and I decided to take our whole family of four children with us for an evangelistic "experience." Upon our arrival at Wonju, we found a little Korean hotel with nice newly papered floors. It was interesting for Naomi and me to notice the reaction of our children as the family settled into the "hotel" room. One child checked out the restroom— sure enough, it was not western style. An older child went to inspect the kitchen, which was below ground level. She saw a lady squatting on the dirt floor chopping vegetables. The rice was cooking in a big pot and would be hot for supper. The boys went out to the courtyard to inspect a Korean Army M.P. jeep. Of course the soldiers were having fun showing the white boys their automatic weapons and other ordnances interesting to boys of any age.

The children liked Korean food and were used to sitting cross-legged around the low round table. The food was hot and enjoyed by the family. Young Glenn ate "keem" (dried sea weed) like it was going out of style. Eloise, the oldest, liked "doc" (rice cakes with sweet bean filling).

After attending the evening meetings, where Lloyd played the little portable organ, the family got out the bedding and prepared to retire. There were no mattresses, just thin pads for each person. Some complained about the hard floor, but at least it was clean. We wanted our children to choose for themselves a future life of service.

George Munson Family
Top row, l to r: Eloise, Naomi, George; Front: Bonnie, Glenn, Lloyd

Chapter 21

HAVE 'G' STRING, WILL TRAVEL
(AKA "GEORGE OF THE JUNGLE" HA!)

In May, 1966, we were called to Sabah, Borneo, north of where I had lived as a teenager, to be Mission president in the area where Naomi's Mother had died of malaria. Not long after Naomi and I made our decision to accept this call, a fellow missionary pulled a trick on us. Ralph Watts sent a telegram from Seoul to Singapore: "HAVE 'G' STRING, WILL TRAVEL," Signed Munson. Everybody had a good laugh. They were being called to Borneo.

We flew to California for a short furlough to visit our two older children, Eloise and Lloyd. Bonnie had spent one year at Rio Lindo Academy and would be finishing at Far Eastern Academy in Singapore. Glenn, our youngest, was not happy about leaving his playmates in Korea and going off to a new place where he would be the only missionary child in that part of Borneo. It was a hard time for him when they flew into Jesselton in September of 1966.

In early April, 1966, I was sent by the Southeast Asia Union Mission to Sabah Mission. The Union officers were holding a meeting there and wanted to introduce me to the wonderful people of Sabah, Malaysia. I spoke to the assembled delegates one morning as Elder Diris Siagian translated for me into the Malay language. I was pleasantly surprised as I listened to the translation. The language came back to my memory like a flood. It had been thirty-two years since I had been exposed to so much Malay. It did not take long to converse with the workers and members, speaking in what the Malaysians call "Bahasa Kabangsa-an" (or national language).

The Union leaders were visiting in the former Mission president's office. I stepped over to the filing cabinet, looked for the financial section and pulled out a recent balance sheet. What a shock to read that the Sabah Mission was $85,000.00

The Sabah mission office was renovated after the termite-ridden material was removed. New bricks and paint made a big difference.

Greeting retired Batak workers who served in earlier years.

Sabah Adventist Secondary School Choir
The director was Linda Sibadogil and she was also dean of Women.

New Boy's Dormitory

in debt. Turning to the treasurer of the Union, I asked, "Is this correct?" What a blow to learn it was true! Right away the officers promised me that they would help solve the problem. Maybe they were afraid I might take the next plane back to Seoul.

Then I was told that the Mission did not have a treasurer. The former man had been dismissed. The position was filled by a retired treasurer, Elder Diris Siagian. I learned that this treasurer had been trained by Lyman Bowers, my dear father-in-law. Brother Siagian was a good man to have during this fiscal crisis. When the Mission board met and suggested spending money, he would ask, "Where is the money for this project?"

There were seven thousand loyal Adventist members attending about 40 churches. We knew that God would help us solve the financial problems if we would obey Him and follow His plan.

We knew, too, that humanly speaking we could not succeed. Prayer bands were organized by the Mission committee for special prayers. We could not move ahead if we did not settle this debt.

Four elementary schools were closed. The publishing department was terminated and all building plans were postponed.

The Mission had already arranged for the purchase of one acre of land with a building on it. The plan was to turn it into a new office building. The old building was termite-ridden and ready to fall down.

There were many positive elements in this new assignment. We ran a successful academy, Sabah Adventist Secondary School. We had a good principal, Edmund Siagian (son of the treasurer) and a very fine faculty. We had fourteen elementary schools to feed this good school.

The Union called Elder Bill Smith and his wife Sue to direct the work in the north section of Sabah, known as Marudu Bay area. He and his wife and three children settled near the town of Bandau, better known by the Adventists as "Goshen".

Elder Anton Waworendeng and his wife Katoo were called from Minehasa to be Mission treasurer and cashier. I had known Katoo when we were children in Minehasa, Sulawesi.

The budget was balanced, one day at a time. There had been plans to renovate the office building but that had to wait. I used a small storeroom in the old office building for a work place. In my files I found letters from people who had made donations in the past. I wrote to them and explained the needs of the Mission. Sometimes funds came to buy a cement mixer and other needed equipment. A doctor in Arizona sent a ski boat with two engines. Someone else sent a check to hold evangelistic meetings or to buy a generator for our school in Goshen. Month by month the Lord sent special funds from friends in America. Relatives sent money to buy bicycles for lay preachers or motorcycles for jungle pastors. In two years we received about US$120,000.00. Some of these contributions were special tithe money. Knowing that the denomination did not permit certain of these funds to be put into the budget, I wrote to Singapore for advice. They encouraged me to use it for evangelism. By 1968 the debt was paid.

We were now ready to build two dormitories for the Academy and also build some churches. Those elementary schools that had been closed were re-opened.

While attending Division committee meetings in the Philippines, I visited a "cement block making" machine factory and bought two machines. This made it possible for the Mission to improve the construction of academies, elementary schools and to upgrade church buildings by solving the termite problem so prevalent in the tropics. At the same time, students could earn their tuition by making these blocks.

Bill and Sue Smith had big plans for the churches in the Marudu Bay district. They upgraded their local school to a full academy and built churches and elementary schools where needed. About 1968 Bill's mother and father came out to visit them in Goshen. Mr. Smith Sr. was an experienced contractor and knew how to give the Mission valuable help as they built the new Goshen Academy. They also built churches and other schools for the Marudu Bay area.

During this time Sue's relative, Dr. McDaniels (a dentist), came to Sabah for a visit. He and Bill went on a jungle medical safari. Pastor Smith had 22 churches in his district. They visited many villages in the Marak Parak district and held village dental clinics in the long houses. They returned with interesting stories and a tin can full of teeth he had pulled--- all eighty of them!

Many of our ministers did not have even high school training. Bill worked out a plan to upgrade these men by meeting with them the last Sunday of each month in one of the churches near the Goshen area, where they discussed problems and received materials. They participated in hands-on demonstrations like how to hold a communion service, "conduct funeral services" or perform a Christian wedding ceremony. The treasurer would then give them their wages and all returned home.

In our next camp meeting ordination, we were able to ordain several men. Some had waited ten years for this honor!

One year there was an epidemic of measles in the area, and 400 babies died. Upon checking with the Bazel Mission Clinic, the nurses there instructed us on how to care for babies and young children who might have measles.

There were three Chinese churches in the Sabah Mission. Elder Chin Kong Loi and his wife were assigned to pastor the church in Jesselton (now Kota Kinabalu), and in Kudat. Elder Tan Peng Hong and his wife were called from Hong Kong to pastor the Sandakan church on the east coast of Sabah.

These men were very helpful in assisting the Mission workers with Ingathering funds. The government would allow us to use the funds for school projects only. One year we gathered $12,000 in Malaysian dollars in Sandakan alone. The Academy students at Tamparuli went out and in one day collected over $6,000. That year our total collection was more than $45,000. Praise the Lord for that gift!

Every year the Chinese businessmen asked why we did not build a hospital in Sandakan. They promised to give liberally to such a project. Finally the Mission committee decided to call an Adventist doctor and ask him to establish a medical clinic in Sandakan and plan to build a hospital later. I wrote to ten Adventist physicians and got one positive answer. Dr. Reginald Rice and his wife Shirley came to serve in Sandakan, Sabah. They were already serving in the Guam Medical Clinic but they left Guam with their three children and came to Borneo. Dr. Rice set up a fine clinic in Sandakan and soon had over 2,000 patients.

The businessmen of Sandakan, who got rich from the mahogany lumber business, kept asking us when we were going to build a hospital. Dr. Rice did some research on acquiring a 10-acre property and drew up plans for a fifty-bed hospital. He found eleven individuals willing to contribute to this building program. The estimate was $600,000 Malaysian dollars. When all was ready the leaders of the Medical Department of both the General Conference and the Union were in the office of the leading businessman in Sadakan. All had gathered to sign the papers so that building could begin. The spokesman picked up his telephone and called the office of the Muslim Prime Minister of Sabah, Dato Mustafa bin Harun. The voice over the phone said, "No mission hospital will be built in Sabah." We were keenly disappointed!

The finances in the Mission had improved. Two dormitories at the Academy located in Tamparuli were completed. We drew additional plans for an auditorium and six new classrooms, utility rooms and restrooms. Back in 1966 we cut off dependence on receiving government funds for building costs and teachers' salaries. This was a wise move, for when the State of Sabah came under Muslim rule, there was no connection with the Department of Education. We were independent.

One Sabbath some high school boys, led by a gangster from Singapore, broke into our Academy treasurer's office and hauled away the safe containing $6,000 in registration fees. They robbed other high school offices, too. The safes were hauled down to the local river, the doors blown off and the contents looted! Then the safes were dumped into the river. It was a rough lesson for our leaders who had not insured the funds lost by theft. The Academy had no security guard system in place; they now immediately set up plans to guard our assets. School boys made rounds to guard the place.

I had worked late at the office, and on my way home I passed between the old office building and the cafeteria. I was swinging my flashlight as I stepped onto the sidewalk. Hearing a loud hiss, I looked over my shoulder and saw a black Malaysian cobra rising up and spraying venom. I turned my head quickly away from the poison spray and ran to the end of the building. Then I walked quickly to the boys dorm to warn the young watchman. The next morning the boys brought to my door a dead black cobra measuring four feet!

Our first camp meeting caused some disappointment because some of the families had to sleep on the ground and it was bad when it rained. When the two dormitories were completed there was room for the families to be under cover. One brother came to me and expressed his pleasure that the girls no longer had to go down to the river to bathe. Later the Michigan Conference sent twenty of their used camp meeting tents. Wooden platforms were made for these tents so even more families were out of the rain..

Most of the churches in the Sabah Mission had only one room with no separate provision for young people or children's Sabbath School. The churches did not have funds to build special rooms for the children. When it rained the kids would squat under the dripping eaves of the church to have their Sabbath School. This was unacceptable. Mrs. Pauline Barnett, Sabbath School secretary of the Southeast Asia Union suggested: "We must have space for the children" and asked the Sabah Mission to pioneer the project she called "Lamb Shelters."

Elder Ginduk Laung was asked to build the first shelter. For US$100 his members built a fine shelter. Our people were delighted and soon we were getting donations for these shelters. Friends and members all over the world supported this program. More than 50 shelters were built in two years. Soon they were building larger buildings and calling them "Jungle Chapels."

The laymen's witnessing program in the Mission was special. In 1968 there was an interest in the student missionary program that was introduced in our Union. Our first student missionary, Charles Eusey (a tall six-foot-six young man from New England) was asked to come for three months and serve our Sabah Mission. His first assignment was in the Goshen area, working with the Kadazan brothers building a palm frond pavilion near Kudat for camp meeting. The workers had a lot of fun watching Charles hand up palm fronds to the roof without using a ladder! When the shelter was finished, we rolled out our bedding on the floor behind the rostrum. We were tired that night as we lay down to sleep. But alas, the fleas weren't. When the campaign was over, Pastor Smith gave Charles the task of teaching a Bible class to a group of 36 students at our school. He said, "I haven't even taught a Sabbath School class." Pastor Smith asked him to prepare these youth for baptism. He rose to the challenge and was proud to stand on the shore of the local river to witness the baptism of his young friends.

We had many enthusiastic laymen who loved to raise up churches in the jungle. Some were converted Shaman priests and former witches. One notable example was Mundahoi. She had inherited witchcraft from her grandmother. She herself became a successful Shaman priestess and was in control of ten villages. She said that she was not satisfied with the power of the jungle spirits, whether evil or good. She heard about a converted priest, Dungko, who was going to speak about the power of the Creator God. She attended the meetings and was deeply impressed with the story of Jesus and His life in Palestine. The Holy Spirit was working on her heart and she asked for special Bible studies. She was very interested in Jesus' work of healing the sick. But first, she wanted to learn how to read the Bible. One of the members gave her lessons on reading the Malay Scriptures called "Al Kitab." Being an intelligent person, she learned fast and went back to her village, Mantub. Her husband was very angry with her. "How can we support our family?" he asked her. When the village chief found out she had become a Christian, he was horrified. He knew for sure the evil spirits would bring on an epidemic on Mantub village!

That night Mundahoi's husband was so angry that he threatened her life. He would not listen to her pleadings and went out to the back yard with his long knife and began to sharpen it on a stone. The frightened children pleaded with their mother to flee for her life. Not knowing what to do, she ran into the darkness of the jungle. As a new Christian she knew of only one thing to do and that was to pray. She fell to the ground sobbing, "Lord, help me. I don't know what to do. I want to be faithful to you but I may lose my life. Hear me, Oh, Lord, in my agony," she prayed throughout that dark, dark night! Spiritual strength came to her as she remembered what she had read in the Bible, "Come unto Me all ye that labor and are heavy laden, and I will give you rest. Take my yoke upon you and learn of me. For I am meek and lowly in heart, and ye shall find rest unto your souls." (Matthew 11:28, 29). As she lay on the ground the peace of God filled her troubled mind. She thought of the marvelous story of Jesus' life she had just heard. About four o'clock in the morning she heard someone calling. As the voice grew louder, she recognized her husband's call. At first she was afraid to answer. He said, "Mundahoi, I forgive you, the children are hungry and crying. We want you back. Please, Mundahoi, come back to your family." Finally she answered and her night of agony was over.

Mundahoi became one of our most enthusiastic lay workers. As the village leaders in Mantub saw the change in her, they grew more positive about this strange event that had taken place in their heathen village. Quietly Mundahoi visited the homes of the sick and prayed for all family members. Forty years earlier, a missionary, Arthur Mountain, had trained the older laymen on how to treat sickness with hot or cold water. He had shown them how to heat up a warm towel and place it on a baby's tummy to relieve colic. He had shown them how to use simple methods to heal family sickness. Using these simple methods, this former witch doctor became a healer for Jesus. She prayed every time she visited the sick and soon the people of Mantub wanted Bible studies, and the little church grew. Now those other villages she had formerly controlled by shaman decrees, ordering chicken or pig sacrifices, did not have the heavy expenses of heathen sacrifices. Instead, she brought the people together to offer Christian prayers to Jesus.

One year when camp meeting was held under a large canopy, nine former shaman priestesses witnessed for Jesus as they told their conversion experiences. Our members were thrilled to hear of God's goodness and power as He helped them raise up churches.

One layman, Brother Sangkee, one of these converted shaman priests, went into the Bandau river watershed country and raised up a church of 25 members. He wanted me to baptize his first converts. Riding in the Mission Land Cruiser, we followed the dirt trail. Finally they arrived at his church.

There had been a drought in the area, so Brother Sangkee was concerned about finding enough water for the baptism. The local stream was almost dry. The only place that had any water at all was a water buffalo wallow nearby with clear, standing water in it. I joined Bill Smith and Sangkee in inspecting the hole. The water was quite clear with a few patches of green scum.

After the worship service in the little thatched church, as I was examining the candidates, it turned out one elderly lady was a former witch doctor. I asked her if she loved Jesus. Her eyes sparkled as she replied, "He has my heart. I was a Shaman priestess most of my life, but I don't want to work for Satan any more. I want to work for God now." They walked to the edge of the pool where the members were gathered singing, "Just as I am, without one plea." I stepped into the water and gently lowered each soul in baptism. After all twelve had been baptized, I lifted my leg onto the bank and pulled off two leeches. I looked up at Brother Sangkee with a knowing smile: "The Lord cares for His own."

Chapter 22

REFUGEES

The Sabah government gave Naomi and me one extra month to pack our belongings and settle our tax debts before leaving the country. Elder Dick Hall, president of Sarawak Mission, had asked me to stop by in Kuching to help them solve a problem with their cement block industry. We stayed at Ayer Manis Academy near Serian. I wanted to see the school that my father had established back in 1933.

Dick drove us to Kuching to the Sunnyhill Academy cement block shop. Observing the production line, I noticed the students were stacking the fresh blocks in the sun without a cover, causing the blocks to dry out too rapidly. Instead of curing properly, they crumbled. We solved the problem by covering the blocks with palm fronds or banana leaves, then moistening them with a fine spray of water to keep them wet for one week to cure.

One day I went with the boys to set up block making on a creek side bank with a good supply of gravel, sand, and water. While making blocks they heard a thud in the forest under a durian tree. The boys jumped up like startled deer and ran for the prize. They brought back this strong smelling, prickly fruit. I suggested that they eat it after they finished their job.

After ten days of stay in Kuching, we booked passage on the steamship "Rajah Brook." Before sailing we visited the old hospital where my Mother's miracle had taken place, and Bao, where as boys Harold and I had visited the Chinese gold mines.

It was very nostalgic to board the ship "Rajah Brook." I was reminded of trips that my family had taken back in earlier days. Now we were leaving Borneo for the last time. As we steamed down the Kuching river, we stood at the rails and prayed that the Lord would be with His people as they faced the difficult times the new Muslim government would bring. We did not realize then that Adventist Christians would lose their jobs and be subjected to the harsh rules of the new government.

Arriving in Singapore, we stayed in the apartment of a missionary couple who were on furlough. The Southeast Asia Union wanted us to hold revival services and teach vegetarian cooking classes in Singapore, then Jahore Baru, Ipoh, Kuala Lumpur and Penang. After Malaysia, we would go to Thailand and present our program in Haadyai, Phuket and Bangkok, finishing in Vietnam with meetings in Saigon and Danang.

As we traveled north towards the Thai border, we were advised to be cautious, for Communist insurgents were operating in the northern jungles. Continuing by taxi, we came upon a Malaysian elephant lumbering along the road. The taxi driver stopped long enough for us to snap a picture of me riding on the elephant. The *mouhat* (elephant keeper) only charged us 4 *baht* (less than $1.00).

Our first destination was on the island of Phuket where we met Jerry and Judy Aitken. As pastor of the church and chaplain at the Adventist hospital, Jerry asked me to speak privately to the nurses. They were Buddhists and declined to join the church, saying they were satisfied with their religion and after all, they were "better than Christians anyway!"

On to Haadyai, we met Dr. Ronald Gregory and his wife who served many years in this hospital. Naomi had attended school with both at Far Eastern Academy when it was located in Shanghai.

The next place was Bangkok, where the church operates a large hospital. The medical work was strong in Thailand, but the membership of the church had not grown like in other places. The Buddhists are proud of their religion and find no need for the Christian faith.

The western border of Thailand was a haven for young people of the Karen tribe living in Myanmar (formerly Burma), who were fleeing from the war. A missionary teacher from Australia had established a school for about 700 youth who wanted to learn and study the English language.

Upon completion of the Thai meetings, we flew east to Phnom Penh, capital of Cambodia. Our plane flew right over the ruins of ancient Angkor Wat. Upon landing in Phnom Penh, we were told: "No one gets off this plane!" Scattered around the airport were wrecks of fighter planes that had been bombed just two days earlier. Antiaircraft guns surrounded the airport and Cambodian soldiers manned them. We were surprised to see women cooking meals and children playing around the guns.

We were to hold meetings in Phnom Penh, but with this critical situation, we decided to fly on to Saigon. As we touched down in Saigon, Brother Pender met us and drove us to his home to visit the hospital and some of the sights of Saigon.

For my first assignment, I conducted a week of prayer for the Academy seniors. Most of the class members came from Communist homes. They sat there whispering to each other and scoffing. So I just smiled and told many stories.

The mission asked us to hold meetings in Danang, where the fighting was still fierce. The local pastor took us to the hotel, surrounded with barbed wire, where the military stayed. We showered in a slimy bathroom and went to bed early. The bed was made of loose boards covered with a sheet. As we dozed off, the sound of heavy military boots in the hall woke us up. A fist pounded on the door. I got up and opened the door a crack. The Vietnamese M.P. demanded to look into the room. I told the police, "My wife is sleeping." He started to shove in the door, but the lady Manager asked me to open the door. When the M.P. saw a white lady sleeping, he left. No "ladies of the night" there!

Our revival meetings were on the weekends. The members had not experienced a Communion service for years. Naomi held a cooking class for the ladies of the church. One day, while I was taking pictures of the class, I stepped out to see what the children were doing. They came around the corner of the building chanting a local ballad. Lo and behold, about six boys were carrying a nine-foot boa constrictor on their shoulders. I went into action, snapping pictures as they marched across the play field. To my consternation, the kids were going to stuff this huge snake into a hole in the wooden well cover, and down into our only drinking water! I protested, so they changed their minds and went marching off. As I came closer for a better picture, I noticed that the serpent's eyes were covered with cataracts. Then I knew why the snake was so docile! He was blind.

The pastor and I rode around on his 90-cc motorbike to visit the church members. I tucked my Bible under my arm, and hung on for dear life to the back of the bike, as we negotiated the paths between the rice paddies. We came to one believer's house which had been demolished by a mortar shell. In the midst of the shambles of their home, they were kneeling behind the sandbagged area and reading from the Scripture, Isaiah 41:10. "Fear thou not for I am with thee, be not dismayed for I am thy God."

That Sabbath was a special occasion as the revival meetings ended with a Communion service. The members came early and traffic was streaming past the little church. I was meditating when suddenly, the sound of gunfire pierced the air. The members ran to the windows to see the show. I was ready to crawl under the pew! Evidently a trigger-happy policeman saw a whole family riding a small Honda motorcycle which was against the law!

The Communion service which followed Sabbath School was a special blessing. Since there were no supermarkets in town with grape juice, it was made by boiling raisins. The bread was not hard to make but the church did not have a Communion service set, so they gathered a lot of little glasses. They were short one cup, so for myself, I took the lid off the kettle and, holding my finger of the steam hole, I poured a small portion for myself. Two Adventist military nurses who were worshiping with us were trying hard to keep from laughing over my creative adaptation.

During the week the Vietnamese pastor took me to comfort a family who lost two children when a rocket demolished their little shelter. We had again come face to face with the awful results of war. The poor people suffer the most when random bombing is used.

With our passports being processed in Saigon, we had no papers to show the authorities in Danang. The Vietnamese M.P. would not let us board the plane. We argued for half an hour until finally I got an idea. I took out my ministerial credential card and wrote my passport number on the card. I took another card out of my wallet and wrote Naomi's passport number on it. The police let us board. We knew the police wanted money, but we refused to bribe.

Arriving in Singapore, we decided to request a permanent return to the U.S. Naomi flew directly to San Francisco to be with Bonnie in college at Angwin.

I flew back to Sabah to finish packing a few personal things and to finish office work in the Mission, for the local people to take over. Edmond Siagian bought our Ford Falcon, and we shipped the rest of our things to San Francisco.

I wondered what I would be doing in the homeland, so I wrote to Northern California Conference inquiring about a job. They answered with the offer of the Petaluma church in California.

We came back to the "new age" of mass media, rapid freeways, rapid transit, jet travel and rapid talk. We were confused by the new roads and speeds that prevailed. The America we had known was GONE! Even buying a new car was a hassle. An Adventist salesman helped us buy a car and a classmate helped us with purchasing furniture. In the mission field the Mission supplied the house and furniture.

We moved into a rental in Rhonert Park near Petaluma. Jerry Wallace, first elder of the church, was a friend from Korean war days.

The church had an active Community Service program. Some ladies were good quilters and distributed a lot of food and clothing to the needy. An active Pathfinder program needed leadership, so in 1972 I took over. We had lots of fun with bike trips, seaside activities, and even a survival camp in the high Sierra mountains. Ira and Effie Stahl invited the church family over to their farm in Cotati for a corn roast. We even had fun with "Ingathering" as several members and youth came out to sing from the back of a pickup, even in the fog!.

We rented a hall in the local park and held bread-making exhibits and cooking classes with Dr Simpson.

By 1973 Effie Stahl had become seriously ill with diabetes. Her condition had degraded to gangrene in her feet and congestive heart failure. So her husband, Ira, requested anointing and a special prayer service at the hospital.

Shortly after this, we accepted a call to Hawaii and lost track on how Effie was doing. While in the islands we received a letter from Ira praising the Lord. Effie had been discharged from the hospital after two weeks, improved in health and lived for seven more years. The Bible says, "Is any of you sick? He should call the elders of the church to pray over him and anoint him with oil in the name of the Lord. Prayer offered in faith will make the sick person well; the Lord will raise him up." (James 5:14, 15).

Chapter 23

PASTORING IN PARADISE

Elder Larry Davidson, president of the Hawaii Conference, called me one day and asked if I would like a second term as pastor of the Waipahu and Waianae churches. Since we had sustained cultural shock working in California, we responded with enthusiasm.

We bought two 8' x 8' containers from a shop in San Francisco, borrowed a truck from a friend, and moved them across the bay by way of the Golden Gate bridge. Fitting our piano and other items into these small containers was a challenge. We finally shipped our household goods and took the airline flight to Oahu. It was good to look down on the hotels of Waikiki and see the crater of Old Diamond Head as the 747 banked around and touched down on familiar soil.

Truly, the Aloha spirit of the island was demonstrated as old friends and officers of the Mission welcomed us with fragrant flower leis. We were happy to set up housekeeping in our new home at 1644 Puananala Street, Pearl City. Soon the freight and auto arrived and we were busy getting settled. Brother Mun On Chang, the Mission treasurer, helped us move the containers to the house. The forklift placed one container on the small truck we had borrowed. Driving towards Pearl Harbour area he turned sharply onto a larger road and, as they turned, the container slid off the metal bed of the truck and fell with a crash to the road. Brother Chang was undaunted. He returned to an airline dock, borrowed a forklift from a friend and soon we were on our way to deliver the load in front of our house.

OPEC, the oil giant of the Near East, was forcing the price and supply of gasoline up and it affected Hawaii, big time. We had just started working with our two churches, Waipahu and Waianae, which were over thirty miles apart. When the gas suppliers started rationing fuel, I got up at 4 a.m. to park in line, listen to "The Haven of Rest," and wait my turn to fill the little blue Chevy. It soon got so bad that Naomi and I packed some clothes and some items of food to eat and slept in the spacious pastor's office in the Waianae church. We finally just moved to Waianae into a nice rental in the Makaha township with 2 ½ acres of tropical fruit trees— mango, macadamia nuts, mountain apples, and we planted six apple banana saplings. It was a great place, but later we found out it was in a tough neighborhood.

Waianae was a very satisfying ministry. The first elder was Lemuel Leialoha. His parents lived in Nanakuli in an area set aside for locals with at least one-quarter Native Hawaiian "blood." We enjoyed the church's rich ethnic mix-- Puerto Rico, Spain, Japan and Europe. They worked well together completing several building projects. A community service and storage. unit was needed, so a block building was built for this purpose. Before leaving Waianae, we helped organize a leeward school in Wahiawa. We had two evangelistic meetings, one in the church and another in the local high school auditorium. Naomi held cooking classes during these efforts.

We were involved with camp meetings and junior camps at Camp Waianae. The Waianae church had a very active Pathfinder club funded by bike-a-thons. The children of the churches of Hawaii were very active in Ingathering.

The Waipahu church was made up of enthusiastic Filipinos who were very loyal to the cause of God. Elder John Klim and his wife Ellen held a very fruitful evangelistic campaign at Waipahu. Ellen Klim is a gifted artist and supported her husband with black light art and music. The church was packed and John and I visited every day to follow up interests. There was great rejoicing as the Lord blessed the church with 39 new souls!

After three years, we were asked to pastor the Diamond Head church (formerly Kaimuki). This was the church that my father, Pastor Albert Munson, had shepherded during the war years when he was also responsible for the Adventist servicemen. The sides of the church were made of doors that could open to a cool garden setting. There were royal palm

Welcomed to Hawaii in 1973

Wainae S.D.A. Church 1973–1976

Waipahu S.D.A. Church 1973–1976

Diamond Head S.d.a.Church 1976–1979

trees with green myrtle ground cover. The light breezes would waft through the church, and the perfume of ginger and gardenia flowers gave a heavenly atmosphere. The music of the Allen organ added to the joy of our worship services.

Brother Wilkes, a converted jazz player from Waikiki, became our Pathfinder director and choir leader. Brother Wilfred Goo, our first elder, was a strong spiritual influence. We sponsored three stop-smoking seminars; the one at Hawaii Kai being the most successful. The Mission van and a Castle Memorial Hospital team held a blood-testing session at the mall entrance. These interests were followed with a stop-smoking seminar held in a boardroom of the mall. There was a lot of fun and joking with the large group of Mormon business people who took the course. I would refer to the "Pearl of Great Price," which is the health manual of the Mormon church, as it admonishes Mormons to not smoke or drink liquor and to eat a vegetable diet.

Mrs. Hazel Sites, the Community Services director, led the ladies in a strong program to help the poor. She kept a good record of those needing help and would arrange for families to get food or clothing, according to their need. The building next to the church was busy during the week.

While serving at the Diamond Head church, the Mission purchased a surplus Navy emergency van equipped with food service appliances, a generator, two-way radio, siren and many other features that made it possible for the Mission to help Civil Defense care for emergency feeding when disaster struck. In 1978, Oahu was struck by heavy storm waves that rolled in from the northwest Pacific. The north shore of the island was hit by thirty-foot waves. One night, Erwin Walker, in charge of the emergency van, called at 2:00 a.m. and asked us to come to help prepare breakfast for victims who were being evacuated to a school on higher ground in that area. We were asked to prepare breakfast for firefighters, rescue workers and local police. We were to be at the Mission office by four o'clock. We jumped into our clothes, slapped a magnetic emergency sign on the Toyota wagon, and raced for the Conference office in Nuuanu Valley. Erwin Walker drove the well-equipped emergency food van to the north shore—siren howling and radio crackling with instructions as to the location for the feeding site.

Within 45 minutes of arriving at the Junior High, we had prepared hot drinks, hash brown potatoes with toast and scrambled eggs. The police and rescue workers were astounded that breakfast was ready so soon. While Naomi and I prepared breakfast, Erwin opened the serving window and set up a table, with plates, cups and hot drink dispenser. When we had served most of the people, I walked down to check out the huge waves rolling in. It was awesome, watching the waves rise up so high and pound the beach with a thunderous roar, taking out landscaping and the front porches of many homes. The people and the rescue team thanked us for the free meal. Later, our Mission emergency van was used in simulated airport disaster exercises by the Civil Defense organization and in real flood emergencies on the island.

Having served in Korea and with a working knowledge of the language, I contacted Korean immigrants in Hawaii and encouraged them to plant a Korean congregation. I gave many Bible studies in Korean and arranged to have Pastor Kim come from the mainland to pastor the small group. The Japanese church very kindly made room in their social hall for the Korean group to worship. This group grew rapidly when Dr. Robert Chung's mother became an Adventist. She was a spiritual pillar to the little congregation.

Some of the most fulfilling years of our ministry were in Hawaii. We helped to lead more than one hundred souls to be baptized. Ben and Elanore Leialoha became lifetime friends. We will never forget the friendly, faithful believers of Hawaii.

Chapter 24

INNER-CITY MINISTRY

In August of 1979, we arrived back in the California Bay area to face the biggest challenge of our forty years of ministry! Back in the Forties and Fifties, Conference leaders had been inspired with the desire to build evangelistic centers in the cities of America. So they built a large church with 1,200 seating capacity in downtown Oakland across from Lake Merit park. On the other side of the lake stood the large Oakland City auditorium which Adventist evangelists rented for meetings with seating capacity for 3,000. The Northern California Conference office was not far away on 14th street. The Conference staff and families and members of the Golden Gate Academy workers helped to fill the new Grand Avenue Seventh-day Adventist church. Elder Tucker, a former pastor, used the mothers' room in the balcony for the broadcasting studio for "The Quiet Hour." Several famous pastors led their congregations in worship in the cathedral-like sanctuary.

But times changed, and when the Conference built a new office in Pleasant Hill, most of the congregation moved away, and with less evangelistic emphasis, the smaller membership could not support large meetings.

By the time we arrived, there were less than 150 active members. In making a demographic study of the East Oakland city, we found there were 4,500 single-parent homes in the area, gang activity existed on many streets, and there were drug pushers just two blocks from the church. However, whether working in the jungles of Borneo or on Fourteenth and Broadway in Oakland, Jesus promised, "Lo, I am with you always, even unto the end of the world." This was our constant security, whether working with drug addicts or homeless people. City pastoring takes patience and "street smarts."

It was a pleasure to work with the pastors of three African-American churches. In 1983, Naomi and I were invited to join Elder George Rainey's evangelistic campaign to be held at the Castlemount High School. This place was like a war zone with the stairwells protected by steel gates. The security guards carried side arms and during meetings, when we took up an offering, they accompanied the deacons to the counting room.

I was in charge of advertising and prepared a large sign with six-foot pictures of Elder Rainey and well known singer "Little Richard," who drew large crowds. In addition to our advertising, we distributed thousands of handbills.

The auditorium seated 1,000 and it was filled every night. The African-American audience especially liked Little Richard's rendition of "Thank You, Jesus." I joined the security guards keeping the area free of druggies.

Laymen and pastors alike were busy visiting interests. With follow-up studies, several Christian ladies we visited were ready for baptism. Many were baptized the last two Sabbaths—the largest group on the last Sabbath. I baptized the two ladies who joined the Grand Avenue church. A total of 150 candidates went into the water where several pastors waited and we sang, "Take Me To The Water."

Early in my ministry at Grand Avenue, board members told me they did not support large evangelistic meetings because they were not cost effective. I said, "You have the wrong pastor." I had held evangelistic meetings during my entire ministry even as publishing house manager in Korea, baptizing more than a dozen people.

We decided to help the church grow by holding vegetarian cooking classes. We arranged the Community Service room so that lectures could be held there.

Chris Chapman and his sister Yvonne, along with Bill and Fred Davis and a few other youth had car washes and they picked and sold fresh fruit to raise money to feed the homeless. They joined with P.U.C. students to give sandwiches to those unfortunates living on the streets of Oakland.

One day the lady in charge of Catholic Charities called and told of a large family of Vietnamese refugee boat people.

Youth and adults help in our V.B.S. with 140 children busses in from
East Oakland.

A group of over 50 attending a cooking class.

Oakland Church Revelation Seminar

Her organization was providing temporary housing for them in a Berkeley apartment house. "Would your church be willing to supply the family with food, clothing, furniture and household goods?" We accepted the challenge and visited the family, finding eight people sitting on the floor wondering what to do. A mother sat on the rug holding a tiny baby wrapped in a towel. The infant was born on the boat they were fleeing in. Our church brought food and cooking pots, towels, clothing, bedding and Asian food like rice and vegetables with which they were familiar.

Since it was Friday, I tried to tell them we would be back on Sunday with a truckload of furniture and household goods. Sabbath I asked the church to donate beds, dressers, divans, tables and other items needed by the family. By Sunday morning we had two pickup truckloads.

Using body language, they expressed deep gratitude for the help. We learned from our experiences with the Vietnamese people that Sears shoes are useless to them. People who have walked barefoot all their lives cannot wear shoes made in this country. Their feet are too w-i-d-e!.

Naomi made up some flash cards and each week she gave several older ladies simple English lessons. Later we helped several youth to learn skills that would help them earn a living in the Oakland area. A member of the church had been injured in an accident. The first elder, attorney Ralph Baker, was handling the case. He asked me to get the Vietnamese to go over to this member's home and repair and paint the interior. A company had just installed a new roof. The Community Service ladies helped clear out the owners' goods. Then we went from room to room, repairing the damaged walls and ceilings, and painting the woodwork, showing the teenagers how to do a good repair job. Later they were able to get jobs repairing homes in the East Oakland area.

Since arriving from Hawaii in 1979, we bought and lived in a three bedroom, two bath home in El Sobrante, near Richmond, California. Naomi's father, Lyman, his sister Cora, his older brother Fred, and younger brother George, were all invited to come and live with us. Uncle Fred and Uncle

George had the master-bedroom, Lyman had his room, and Aunt Cora had the corner bedroom.

The double garage was carpeted for a special living space, so Naomi and I converted it into an apartment for us. Half was office, and the other half was a bedroom.

The senior siblings were in their late eighties and early nineties. They enjoyed so much being together. Everyone was happy and content.

Naomi was busy keeping this group fed and their laundry washed. But (bless her heart) every Tuesday afternoon she would jump in the car with me and visit church members and give Bible studies to families in East Oakland. This house had a large patio and well-landscaped yard. I couldn't resist putting a redwood deck under some large Monterey pines.

Another blessing we had in the Grand Avenue church was the family of Fred and Mary Tsujimura. For years they had invited people to their Victorian home on East 23rd street. With gracious Asian hospitality they provided Sabbath lunch for many people. After lunch there would be singing around the piano in the living room. One Sabbath the youth gathered there and had a "rap session." "What could we do to help our church program?" In 1983, when the President declared the "Year of the Bible," the youth conducted a Bible Fair with interesting booths on archeology, the days of creation, a Bible study video center for children, a special Bible display of very old Bibles, and a parlor setting where people could ask questions and get answers. The finale was a movie on John Wycliffe, the great Bible translator. More than 75 visitors came to this beautiful exhibit. Every 7th, 12th and 40th visitor received a book prize.

Jo-Ann (Tsujimura) and Gerald Johnson and their children were a blessing with Jo-An as George's capable secretary and church organist. Gerald was our church deacon and their two children, Julie and Gerald Jr, were active youth. The church had a very active choir and it enhanced our worship services.

There were several funerals in those years but the most tragic event was the untimely death of Paul Cortese. All mourned deeply as they sought to comfort the family. His wife Arlene, with the help of the family, commissioned the art department of Rio Lindo academy to craft a beautiful faceted glass window with the theme "The Coming of Jesus in Glory." In the dark foreground you see the Bay Bridge lights and in the background the famous Golden Gate string of lights. Above are the angels descending from heaven and our dear Saviour sitting on a cloud of glory. On that glorious day we will meet our dear ones as they come out of their graves.

Not very many people knew Annbelle Jones. She was a trained nurse but who quietly ministered to the pain and suffering of many of Jesus' children in the West Oakland area. Even though her own husband was ill and later died, she did not stop her ministry, She truly was a saint and a "Mother in Israel." There were so many wonderful people in this congregation. What a joy it will be to see them in the Kingdom.

Often I prayed about the slow progress of the church and dreamed of turning Grand Avenue SDA church into an international congregation. Some folks were unhappy about this dream, but the board finally gave permission to invite the Hispanic congregation (that had been worshipping in a storefront) to worship in the social hall. There they had a platform, a pulpit, curtains and plenty of chairs and even an organ and piano. There were 55 members who enjoyed this fellowship and they joined us for Communion. They showed us how to grow a congregation. They held two public evangelistic meeting each year, inviting Spanish-speaking evangelists to lead out in their campaigns. Each family brought their non-Adventist friends and loved ones to the meetings in their own cars. In two years they had grown to almost one hundred members. It was a joy to worship with them and join in their Sabbath fellowship dinners held on the green grass of Lake Merit park. These wonderful brothers and sisters reflected what they had experienced in Central and South America and were a real inspiration and example.

On May 15, 1984, Naomi and I retired from active duty. We still join in witnessing activities, even though our strength has diminished and our footsteps are not as sure. Our hearts will always be in Asia. We were born and raised there and spent twenty-five years in active overseas service. Our mission service, in Sabah, Borneo and in Korea, was exciting and challenging! We are happy to have joined cousin Samuel Munson and his fellow missionary in preaching the gospel in Asia. Munson and Lyman paid the supreme price of death at the hands of cannibals in the jungles of Sumatra. They were inspired by the words of the Apostle Paul in Romans 8:35–37, "Who shall separate us from the love of CHRIST? Shall tribulation, or distress, or persecution, or famine, or nakedness, or peril or the sword? As it is written, For Thy sake we are killed all the day long; we are accounted as sheep for the slaughter. Nay, in all these things WE ARE MORE THAN CONQUERORS, THROUGH HIM THAT LOVED US."

Tombstone of Samuel Munson and Henry Lyman, 1834

MISSION IN PADANG 1900–1905

In 1900 R. W. Munson pioneered as a self-supporting missionary in Indonesia.

Ralph Munson Memorial church built in 1985 by members of the Padang Church in Sumatra.

This marble plaque is in the memorial church in Padang.

The George Munson Family
Glenn, Eloise, Naomi, Lloyd, George, Bonnie

EPILOGUE

Our children shared in mission service overseas alongside their parents. They suffered the pain of disease and its effect on their bodies. They felt the sting of reproach when maligned by local nationals. Some missionary children paid the supreme price and lie in lonely graves across Asia. They also shared the joy of seeing souls saved and victories won for the work of God. Each cherishes the friends made in foreign lands. They learned local languages and contributed to mission projects. They may have been deprived of the education that many home-based children get, but they enjoyed first-hand experience in world geography and cross-cultural human relations. They learned patience and how to adapt when difficulties arose.

Ruth Eloise Munson was born December 28, 1942, in St. Helena, California, in the beautiful wine country of Napa Valley. A few days later, Naomi and I brought her to the little home we had built at 40 Diogenes Drive in Angwin.

The Missions had established grade schools for mission children and provided teachers to operate the schools. The Far Eastern Division established a good Academy in Singapore so the missionaries' children would experience higher education with classmates from similar backgrounds.

After finishing eighth grade, Eloise took ninth grade at home by correspondence. Then Naomi and I had to say goodbye to their beautiful teenage daughter as she flew to Far Eastern Academy in Singapore.

Eloise grew up having artistic talents. One of her college teachers was Vernon Nye, who specialized in water color. He taught his students to take bold strokes with their brushes and to be more creative in style and use of color.

Later Eloise used this talent to teach art and Interior Design in elementary school, high school and college. She has used her talents to decorate her own home and pursued her ambitions as a professional interior designer. The results of her work can be seen in many buildings at Loma Linda and other Southern California institutions.

Eloise met Todd Murdoch at F.E.A. in Singapore. His parents, Todd and Jean Murdoch, served the Lord for many years in the Philippines. Eloise and Todd studied at P.U.C. and were married in Dauphinee Chapel one week after graduation. After serving in the business office at P.U.C., Todd became the treasurer of San Fernando Valley Academy. Later he was called to Loma Linda University School of Dentistry and served for many years as Associate Dean for Financial Administration. He is currently the President of La Loma Federal Credit Union in Loma Linda.

Eloise continued her career in teaching Interior Design and Art, acquiring a Lifetime Teaching Credential for Interior Design from the State of California. With her Bachelor of Science degree in Interior Design from P.U.C., she became the design coordinator for many facilities such as Loma Linda University and Medical Center, Glendale Adventist Medical Center, White Memorial Medical Center and the Islands of Guam and Saipan Mission Clinics. She has designed many church interiors, waiving her fee as a thank you to the Lord for all He has done for her and her family. She is now the Project Manager for La Loma Federal Credit Union's new building construction. They have lived in Loma Linda more than thirty-five years and they have two children: Todd and Tonya.

May 3, 1944, just one month before I graduated from P.U.C., Lloyd Irving was born at St. Helena Hospital. So I have always said "I got two degrees that graduation day—a scholastic B.A. and a paternal P.A." But they called me "Dae, Dae" or just "Dad."

Lloyd inherited many talents and enjoyed the out of doors, whether climbing trees, whittling wood, drawing pictures or just teasing.

When our family sailed from Yokohama, Japan, for our 1953 furlough, I wondered what to buy to keep my children busy on board the ship "Flying Dragon." I stopped at a hobby shop in Tokyo and bought a foot-long 2 x 4 of balsa wood, some sandpaper and razor blades. After the usual family tradition of looking over the ship, Lloyd settled down to carve a model of the ship. In the hallway was a picture and plan of the vessel. We downsized the dimensions from that blueprint. Several days later we met the captain in the dining room and showed him the model Lloyd had carved. It had tiny masts, superstructure with lifeboats and other gear, and even a little rudder. The captain was so pleased he wrote a note to the ship's carpenter and ordered him to give us the actual paint used on the ship.

His senior year at Pacific Union College, Lloyd found his life companion, Jeanne Kurtz, daughter of Arnold Kurtz and Carol (Wallace) Kurtz. Arnold pastored the East Oakland S.D.A. church just prior to Lloyd and Jeanne's being married there. Both Arnold and I officiated at the wedding. Arnold and Carol have spent 25 years in pastoral/evangelism and 15 years teaching at Andrews University.

Lloyd's first assignment was Associate Pastor of the Santa Rosa church for a year and then on to Andrews University, where he eventually earned his Doctor of Ministry Degree.

With his training, and Jeanne by his side (with her musical talent) he pastored eleven churches and taught Bible in three academies and three of those years as a fourth-generation missionary in Singapore and Japan). He and Jeanne pastor the Aiea church in Hawaii, the same church started by his father, George, and his grandfather, Albert, sixty years earlier (July 7, 1947).

Bonnie June Munson was born in Seoul, Korea, on June 1, 1949. We called her "*Mi Ja*" in the local language, which means "Beautiful Child." She became a refugee at one year of age as the family had to flee from the North Korean Communist armies. They fled to Japan where she lived in a new culture for three years.

Bonnie is naturally a kind, loving and tender-hearted person. As a child she was always taking care of playmates who got hurt. As an adult she worked with Home Health as a nurse's assistant, helping people who could not help themselves.

Like her siblings, she was blessed with artistic talent, inherited from her grandpa Albert and her great-grandpa Harry Chatterton.

In order for Bonnie to attend her sister's wedding, she needed to spend one year attending school in America, so she enrolled at Rio Lindo Academy. There she met Mike Hunter. The next year she was back at F.E.A. After graduating, she enrolled at Pacific Union College. Later she married Mike and they settled in his hometown of Mt. Shasta. Later they divorced.

With her smile and cheerful attitude, she makes friends easily. Bonnie is now happily married to Jeremiah Keyes, a retired Santa Rosa fireman.

Bonnie enjoys her work at the Credit Union and staying in touch with her four adult children: Hiedy Anna; twins, Alethea and Allana; and Michael, also known as Mike or "Bud."

Glenn Innes Munson, our youngest son, was born April 22, 1954, while the family was home on furlough. He was also born at the St. Helena Sanitarium and Hospital. In his newborn state, he did not realize that his future wife would be born at the same hospital the following year. At three months, Glenn traveled with the family back to South Korea where he grew up and made many friends in both Korea and Borneo.

With his parents' encouragement, he replaced friends with pets such as monkeys, Gibbon apes, ducks, snakes, a flying lizard, a goat, turtles, and his favorite—a pigtailed baboon named Harry. Would he become a zookeeper?

Glenn's Junior High education began at home in Northern Borneo, doing home study with Mom's tutoring. He then left home at age 14 to attend Far Eastern Academy in Singapore. Three years later he moved on to attend Pacific Union College Prep School in Angwin, California, graduating in the spring of 1972.

Pacific Union College accepted his application in the fall of that same year. Glenn's work on the Campus police force taught him how to stay out of trouble! At the end of the first quarter of his third year at college, while standing in line at the college cafeteria, Glenn met his wife-to-be, the "all-grown-up" baby girl, Carol Lynette Wilson, born at St. Helena Hospital, October 27, 1955. Carol has connected some family history that he knew nothing about. She informed him that his grandmother, Katherine Innes-Munson, was her mother's chaperone aboard ship from Sydney, Australia, to the United States in 1949.

Glenn's musical talent extracted him from schoolwork the second quarter of his junior year to sing with Bill Truby's Evangelistic outreach group "The Sound of Care." They traveled the U.S. West Coast, including Hawaii.

I, George Munson, had the privilege of marrying Glenn and Carol in Modesto, California, December 21, 1975.

Inheriting the creative, artistic genes of the Munson Clan, Glenn was led to the profession of Dental Lab Technology, working in the Modesto/Ceres area. His second interest was ministering to young people, which led him to heed the call of God to the Ministry.

Glenn and Carol moved to Southern California where he graduated with a B.A. in Theology from La Sierra College. Anaheim Adventist Church then selected Glenn to be their Youth Pastor, with his eventually taking over as Senior Pastor within the year.

After two years in Michigan to complete his Master of Divinity Degree at Andrews University, they returned to Southern California where Glenn took up the duties of Youth Pastor at the Riverside Adventist Church while Carol continued her education at Loma Linda School of Nursing, graduating with the R.N. Degree. Glenn and Carol have ministered to churches in California and Oregon and currently reside in Yucaipa, California. He shepherds the congregation at Point Loma, near San Diego. They have two sons: Rick and Ryan.

A TRIBUTE TO MY SIBLINGS

Harold was full of talent and had great creativity. He inherited the special knack of catching facial expressions and body language that made his art work so meaningful and true to life. He has illustrated over 400 books.

He and Arla, his wife, raised four daughters who enjoyed his love of storytelling and singing the ballads of his native Indonesia.

During his teenage days, Harold was taken by Pappa Albert to many high school art classes, and they learned together.

Later he worked in the art departments of Lockheed Corporation, Pacific Press Publishing Association, and Review and Herald Publishing Association. During his retirement, he continued to produce a large volume of art work (of which we have examples in this book). After Arla's death, he married Carlotta Schuett, a long-time secretary at the Voice of Prophecy. It was a beautiful wedding in Monterey Bay and she was a good companion for him. As he became more dependent, she lovingly cared for him.

Iva Munson-Baasch was born in Java and married David Baasch, son of a missionary family from South America. They spent many years working in Spanish-speaking countries like Colombia, Puerto Rico and Mexico. Finally, he was called to the General Conference to direct the South American work of the church.

While they were in Washington, Iva taught in the J. N. Andrews Elementary school. After David's death, she retired and served in several overseas assignments, beginning in Indonesia's English Language School in Bandung; next at Mission Elementary School in Bangkok, Thailand; and lastly at the Grianach School in Galway, Ireland.

She has four children: Gwendolyn, Harold, Cathy and David.

Paul Munson was born in Manado, Indonesia and the whole family enjoyed having a baby in the home. He still enjoyed living at home with his folks in Hawaii and attended Hawaiian Mission Academy during World War II and following.

Paul received his Degree in Graphic Arts from CalPoly in San Luis Obispo, California.

He has a distinguished record in serving Dow Jones Corporation in San Francisco, California; Dallas, Texas; New York; Winnetka and Naperville, Illinois. His wife Barbara works in real estate.

Paul and Barbara raised two children: Christie and Scott. They now enjoy a delightful retirement fellowship in the Cambria Presbyterian Congregation of Coastal Southern California.

We'd love to have you download our catalog of
titles we publish at:

www.TEACHServices.com

or write or email us your thoughts,
reactions, or criticism about this
or any other book we publish at:

TEACH Services, Inc.
254 Donovan Road
Brushton, NY 12916

info@TEACHServices.com

or you may call us at:

518/358-3494